# *Birdwatch Around Scotland*

## W. R. Mitchell

ROBERT HALE · LONDON

For
PETER DELAP

who loves wild, remote places

© W. R. Mitchell 1983
*First published in Great Britain 1983*

ISBN 0 7090 1248 9


Robert Hale Limited
Clerkenwell House
Clerkenwell Green
London EC1R 0HT


Photoset by Rowland Phototypesetting Ltd
Printed in Great Britain by
St Edmundsbury Press, Bury St Edmunds, Suffolk
Bound by Hunter and Foulis Ltd

# CONTENTS

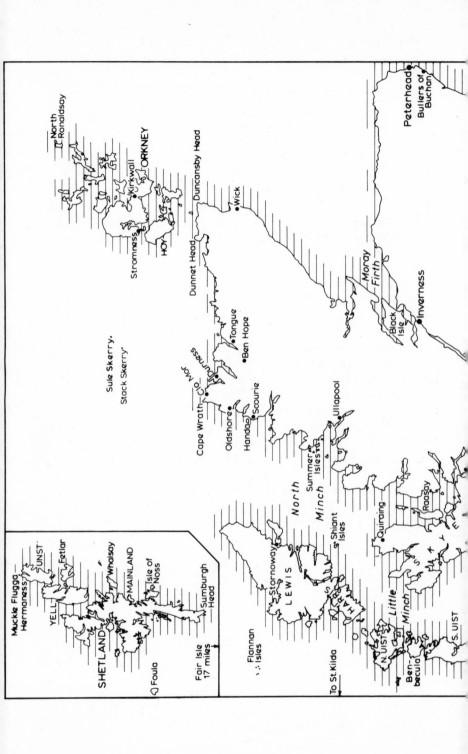

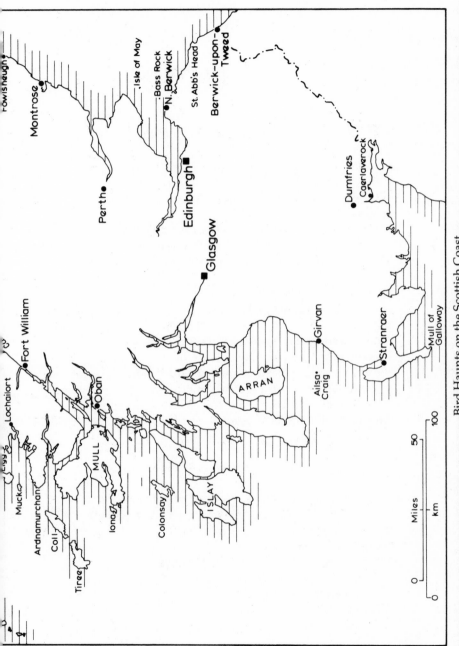

Bird Haunts on the Scottish Coast

Fowlsheugh
Montrose
Perth
Isle of May
Bass Rock
N. Berwick
St. Abb's Head
Berwick-upon-Tweed
Edinburgh
Glasgow
Dumfries
Caerlaverock
Fort William
Lochailort
Eigg
Muck
Ardnamurchan
Coll
Tiree
MULL
Iona
Oban
Colonsay
ISLAY
ARRAN
Girvan
Ailsa Craig
Stranraer
Mull of Galloway

Miles
km
0        50        100
0

# ILLUSTRATIONS

All unacknowledged photographs were taken by the author.

The air was dirkit with the fowlis,
That cam with yammeris and with yowlis,
With shrykking, screeking, shrymming scowlis,
And muckle noyis and showtes.

*William Dunbar*

# An Introduction

*Viking, Forties, Cromarty, Forth, Tyne* . . . The radio announcer broke into my early morning reverie with details of the shipping forecast. *Rockall, Hebrides, Bailey, Fair Isle* . . . The names given to Scottish coastal waters unlocked memories of islands and sea lochs, headlands and dunes, from Muckle Flugga to the Mull of Galloway. *Tiree, Sumburgh, Bell Rock* . . . Reports from coastal stations induced further recollection, this time of bird life. Manx shearwaters performed an aerial ballet off the Small Isles. Puffins, dumpy and dark against the sea's glare, swarmed like bumble-bees at Noss and Hermaness. Guillemots jostled each other on the redstone ledges of Handa. Gannets – 'the white birds of the herring' – dived like meteorites above shoals of herring or mackerel, drawing their wings to their sides a second or two before touching the sea.

This book is a celebration of Scotland's diverse, hauntingly beautiful coastline and its avian riches. It is mainly about seabirds, but who could ignore the corncrake I met on the wild Sutherland coast? The whimbrels displaying above their moorland territories on the northern isles had sea views all around them. A red-necked phalarope nesting in a marshy place on Fetlar would spend eight months of the year on the ocean waves. The barnacle geese at their Inner Solway roost would start the night with their webbed feet planted firmly on a sandbar and greet the dawn while paddling on a flow tide.

The seabird colonies distinguish Scotland in the context of European wildlife. Each spring, millions of seabirds arrive at the cliffs and stacks. As the sun climbs and the sea blooms – offering food for all – a myriad birds display, copulate, brood eggs and feed chicks. When these birds and their young have gone, millions more birds – refugees from the Arctic winter – arrive on the Scottish coast and islands. Some birds refuel during longer journeys; others linger in favourable areas until the impulses of

11

migration coax them northwards again. The gales which exhaust bird-travellers, or throw them off their usual course, are welcomed at bird observatories such as Fair Isle and the Isle of May, where such autumn 'exotics' are logged. Fair Isle has recorded hoopoe, short-toed lark, yellow-breasted and little buntings, even the nightingale. Almost two hundred species of bird might be captured, ringed and released in a single season.

The Scottish coastline has infinite variety. In the far south, near the Mull of Galloway, the North Atlantic Drift laps against a landscape which is consequently tolerant towards tropical plants. The northern islands – those stepping-stones leading from the Scottish mainland towards Norway – cross the 60th parallel, have few trees and their own special varieties of cabbages. Most of Shetland lies as far north as Cape Farewell in Greenland, and local people sunbathe wearing jumpers with the sleeves rolled up!

Ardnamurchan, not Land's End, is the most westerly point on the British coast. Ardnamurchan points a gabbro-tipped finger towards the Hebrides, the enchanted isles – a chain extending for almost 300 miles, from Ailsa Craig, which adorns the Clyde like an upturned pudding-basin, to North Rona, a speck of land in the North Atlantic. The Hebrides face over 2,000 miles of open sea with shell-sand beaches, cliffs of granite and gabbro, and the machair-lands, herb-rich sward behind the dune systems. When the machair blooms in June and July, it has the floral richness of alpine meadows. Charlock, corn marigold, storksbill and pansy, in dense carpets, light up the landscape.

To the Norsemen, who dominated life in the West for four centuries, the Outer Hebrides were the 'isles at the edge of the sea'. There are remoter places, further west. St Kilda, an island group some 50 miles west of Harris, confronts the sea with awesome cliffs and stacks. One of the cliffs is over a quarter of a mile high. Over 180 miles from St Kilda, the sea creams against a solitary stack, Rockall, the Gaelic name for which means 'sea rock of roaring'.

The Western Isles, scattered remnants of an ancient landscape flooded by the sea, are Sunset Islands. In the West, for every well-known island like Lewis or Skye there are dozens of insignificant plots: Sula Sgeir and Sule Skerry, named after the gannet; Rona and Skerryvoe; Dubh Artach and Muck. Far to the south, on

Islay, choughs may be seen around the Mull of Oa, and the autumn air tingles with the cries of wild geese, barnacles and white-fronts. Far to the north, Shetland's 100 isles total 552 square miles. An English visitor who has made the long journey to Sutherland is chastened to discover that the name comes from the Norse *sudr*, meaning south land. A Shetland health visitor told me she was going 'south' for her main holiday. She intended to visit friends in Edinburgh, which would involve a long journey.

Western Scotland, against which the Atlantic rollers spend their energy, is the wettest – and most midge-ridden – part of Britain, though its reputation for foul weather is not always deserved, and if you go in spring you may cheat the midges. (Look out for the sheep-ticks!) When the wind is roaring, a dustbin may be blown from one side of the house to the other, and the slates go up and down like piano keys.

Scotland faces the North Sea with cliffs, dunes and muddy inlets. The north coast overlooks the Pentland Firth, reputedly the stormiest stretch of water in Britain, a battleground of tidal rips. From Cape Wrath, there is open sea from Scotland to the North Pole. At Caithness, the scouring tide has eroded a sandstone coastline, leaving lofty stacks. (The name 'stack', used to describe an isolated column, is yet another legacy of the Vikings, deriving from the Norse *stakkr*.)

Dr Johnson said to a proud Scot: 'Your country, sir, consists of two things, stone and water.' The coastal flavour extends far inland as sea or freshwater lochs. A dedicated Scot calculated that there are over 9,000 lochs of appreciable size away from the coast. In places the landscape has a half-drowned appearance. There are far more birds than people. A sea eagle takes to the air on wings spanning eight feet; it is as though a barn door has become airborne. At the other end of the scale are the six-inch-long phalaropes, the young of which are so small and dainty they have been described as 'bumble-bees on stilts'.

Bird calls are like echoes from the dawn of time. Divers wail. Storm-petrels purr. Shearwaters scream. Arctic skuas mew, fulmars cackle, whimbrels titter, puffins growl and the black guillemot – the little tystie – whistles. A traveller finds himself among a bird-conscious people. I was charmed by bird names used in Shetland: 'maalie' for fulmar, 'mootie' for storm-petrel, 'scarf' for shag, 'Tammie Norie' for puffin, 'tirrick' for tern.

Forty years have gone by since I first watched birds on the Scottish coast and began to study the writings of many first-rate Scottish observers of birdlife. Books written by Frank Fraser Darling had a special appeal. He had experienced what he wrote about. When many naturalists were poring over specimens in dusty studies, Darling used the outdoors as his laboratory. He wrote with simple clarity, with a fine turn of phrase. While on the Summer Isles, he mentioned the seething, toiling bird life, 'this short summer glory of light, colour and activity'. I met my hero once – and I said not a word. He was sitting at the next table when the British Deer Society had its annual meeting in Perth. He leaned over and asked, with courtesy and charm: 'May I parasitise you?' We were drinking tea at the time. He merely wanted to borrow the sugar basin!

It was the daily litany of the shipping forecast that led to my mental stocktaking of experiences at the rim of Scotland and prompted me to write this book. Here is one man's selection of bird haunts. The descriptions are detailed enough for any interested reader to seek out the wild places. But first we meet some of the seabirds and consider man's relationship with them over several thousand years . . .

# 1

# When the Sea Blooms

Long before the Old Year is out, there is a stir at the coastal cliffs. Fulmars appear, cutting the air with stiff, straight wings, surveying all through dark eyes. These Scottish birds are paler, larger-nebbed, than are their high-Arctic cousins, which glide to the edge of the pack-ice. Winter visits to the nesting cliffs occur in fine weather. As another gale advances – as the sea explodes against the rocks – the fulmars depart for a while. Soon they are back, gaping and cackling on every stretch of coast from Unst to Galloway, from Cape Wrath to St Abbs Head.

A stiff wind brings out the best in the fulmar. The bird glides with scarcely a wingbeat, conserving its energy as it quests for food over the ocean. James Fisher called the fulmar 'this grey ghost glider of stormy seas'. The bird exploits the updraught from the waves; it twists and soars to avoid yet another wall of foam-frilled water, and when it returns to the cliffs, it hangs on the wind, with dangling legs and fanned tail feathers, or goes on patrol, seemingly interested in everything that stirs.

The young birds flew only a matter of weeks before the first of the adults returned to loiter at the nesting sites. '*Fúll már*,' grunted the Norseman. The name means 'foul gull', an allusion to its musky odour. When St Kilda was the only British nesting station of the fulmar, it might be seen in November, when according to Martin Martin (1698) it was 'the sure messenger of evil tidings'. The fulmar brought with it 'boistrous W. winds, great snow, rain or hail . . .' This is the only European petrel with the temerity to visit land during the day.

The 'penguins of our northern seas' may also visit the cliffs out of season. Some guillemots and razorbills are back after an interval of only two months. In July they had escorted their young to the fishery off the coast of southern Norway. The young loitered or even went further north, while the adults took a southwards course, making a broad circuit of the North Sea, back

15

at their nesting colonies in good time to occupy a cliff's vacant lots. The auks appear close to the cliffs in the early morning; they are nervous about settling on land, and the least disturbance sends them whirring back to sea, where they swim buoyantly or dash about underwater, enveloped in air bubbles, using their short, stiff wings for propulsion.

Young gannets that took their first wavering flights in the early autumn are now far away, plunge-diving for fish off the west coast of Africa or in the Mediterranean. By January, the first of the adult birds are back at their nesting islets. They scan the cliffs of Hermaness and Noss, Bass Rock and Ailsa Craig. They re-colonate Sula Sgeir – 'sula' from the old name for gannet – which is a rockscape forty miles north of the Butt of Lewis, from which men sail in autumn to cull the *gugas* and to preserve them as food.

Eiders, plump and round, assume their breeding plumage as they frequent rocky stretches of the coast, where beds of blue mussels sustain them when they are hungry. The male eider is white on top, dark beneath, reversing the conventional colour scheme among waterfowl. In February, oystercatchers – the dandies of the tideline – tenant the lonely shore and prospect here and up the river systems for nesting territories. Oystercatchers return to the northernmost isles, flaunting their bright plumage and making the air ring with their strident piping.

On the machair, a lark rises, brimming over with song. Lapwings call as they tumble, floppy-winged, in the early spring breezes. Curlews climb with powerful wingbeats, set their trim for gliding and drift earthwards with bubbling trills. When the old whaup is back in its nesting area, the worst of the winter is surely over! A few kittiwakes were in home waters in January; the crowds return by March, rousing the dormant echoes between high rock faces. The North Atlantic is the kittiwake's parish. Back on land, the birds are on the ledges by day but roosting on the sea at night, until the nesting fever is on them, when they cling to their nest sites – improbable-looking knobs and ledges well clear of the sea's splash-line.

Guillemots let off steam; they dance on the sea with pattering feet. They dive in boisterous groups, using their wings as oars, their feet as rudders, as they cavort in the green water. By Easter, black-throated and red-throated divers are back at their breeding lochs in north-western Scotland and the isles. The black-throats select the largest stretches of water; the red-throats make do with hill lochans, commuting to the sea to feed. Birds that were silent on the steel-grey ocean now keep up a loud wailing, the sound reverberating between the orange-banded hills.

Manx shearwaters, in flickering flight off the islands, turn to reveal, first, the dark upperparts, then the white underparts. As darkness falls, the shearwaters assemble in rafts, rising and falling with the waves, like patches of weed. When it is truly dark, the shearwaters rise to fly to their nesting burrows, and the night air fills with their screams and cackles. They circle the Rhum coolins; others skim the boulder slopes of Car Mor, on St Kilda. Black guillemots – the 'tysties' of Scotland – indulge in fast and fanciful water sports before stationing themselves near the stretches of rocky shore where nesting will take place. The first of the returning 'tysties' have wintry white on their plumage but soon moult into a smart black, with white wing patches. The birds come ashore, moving with curious mincing steps, displaying the bright red of their legs.

The clarion call of herring-gulls is heard from cliff and skerry, from urban chimney-pot or the top of a building near a busy harbour. At Mallaig, the buildings appear to be thatched with feathers. Gulls wail mournfully from the chimney-pots of Lerwick, in Shetland. Some of the returning lesser black-backed gulls have not travelled far; they joined herring-gulls at the corporation rubbish tips. Yet more return from wintering quarters in Iberia or North Africa. With deep barking, the great black-backed gulls claim territories on the stacks and islets, where the summer menu will consist partly of seabirds, taken dead or alive.

The returning skuas – which a Shetlander described as 'the sharks of the sky' – infuse the dark northern landscape with a sense of life after the winter stillness. Great skuas, the 'bonxies', and their smaller cousins, the Arctic skuas, followed the migrating seabirds southwards, harassing them, forcing birds to disgorge their last meals, then losing themselves in the Atlantic until the lengthing days triggered off the responses that would lead to breeding, coaxing them northwards to the isles. Puffins appear off the coastal cliffs; they pay erratic, nervous visits to the jumbled rocks or grassy slopes where their burrows are to be found. Puffins touch down hesitantly at Hermaness and Noss, Clo Mor, St Abbs and dozens of other nesting stations. Thousands of puffins congregate on the Flannan and Shiant Isles and, when taking off to feed, work their short, stiff wings so vigorously that they seem in danger of breaking off. The terns proclaim their return to the nesting grounds with creaky voices. Much less conspicuous are the storm-petrels and Leach's petrels, vanguards of the seabird host, which pay nocturnal visits to a cluster of outlying islands, where they nest in crannies.

The sea blooms. For weeks it will offer an inexhaustible bounty to millions of seabirds, which regulate their nesting programmes to the period of plenty. Spring merges imperceptibly into summer. On the northern isles, it is the time of the "simmer dim", when it is never really dark. Minute forms of plant life, the phytoplankton, are energized by the sun, nurtured by the nutrients in the upper layers of the sea, where tropical water mixes with cold currents from the Arctic. The plant material feeds the zooplankton. Countless millions of fish eggs contribute to the thin soup of the sea as it responds to warmth and bright light.

The nutrients are stirred as ocean currents and water from the rivers merge and mix over the shallow continental shelf, to be further agitated by tidal rips, by the surge of the sea around stack and headland. Plankton provides food for a host of creatures. Fish are nurtured and thrive. Seabirds seek out the fish – auks after sprats and sand-eels, gannets after herring and mackerel, which begin to move inshore about midsummer. Tysties take small fish, crustacea and mollusca from close to the rocks. Cormorants submerge and pursue fish with powerful strokes of their webbed feet. The birds surface, to stand on rock perches, opening their sodden wings to sunshine and breeze.

Fulmars scoop up zooplankton and fish guts from trawlers; kittiwakes take both plankton and fish. Shearwaters hover or dive on young fish. Skuas descend on the fish-eaters and take their food second-hand. Storm-petrels flutter and glide like tiny bats, taking plankton and the smallest fish. Gulls, in screaming hordes, follow the homecoming trawlers and descend on the jettisoned scraps of fish.

The sky and sea are blue; sunlight makes the ancient cliffs gleam; acres of sea pinks bloom – and the seabirds, in clamorous throngs, go through the nesting ritual in a way that assails the senses of a human visitor. There is colour, non-stop movement, harsh calling, a cloying smell. The action spreads across the sea, where rafts of birds fish or rest or preen. Guillemots spring from a frothing sea to climb sheer slopes, their whirring wings giving them extra power and stability as they seek out resting-places. The high concentration of birds is possible because there is food for all, with no need to bicker over it. There is safety in numbers; the theme song might be: "The more we are together, the happier we shall be."

On the dunes, eiders cover their eggs, which are swaddled in down. Gulls nest by the thousand, with the nests spaced at the limits of tolerance. Terns are garrulous and restless – sprightly 'sea swallows', uttering grating cries as they jerk their way across the sky. Many terns have wintered in the tropics. The Arctic tern commuted between Scotland and the Antarctic and on its return to the north for nesting had flown a round trip of some 25,000 miles.

The cliff-nesters occupy every reasonable site. Just above the splash-mark are the tysties and the shags. Guillemots pack the higher ledges, growling at each other, jabbing with their spear-like bills at intruders. Razorbills are among the boulders or in the crannies. Fulmars squat on every convenient ledge. Gannets, occupying the major ledges, make nests that are like mini-volcanoes. Puffins colonize the grassy tops of cliff and stack.

A flush of eggs appears. Many eggs will be lost. Enough will survive to ensure the continuation of the species. The fulmar sits on a single, coarse white egg. The gannet keeps its single, pale blue egg warm beneath its webbed feet. Single eggs are more the rule than the exception. The guillemot's egg is large and phyriform, deposited on rock, where a quite 'jazzy' colouring is soon marked by guano – which also has the merit of helping it to stay put on its windswept ledge. Rather less colourful is the egg of the razorbill, tucked out of sight in a rock crevice or among boulders. The puffin's egg is white; no cryptic colouration is needed, for it reclines in a hole. The Manx shearwater's egg lacks colour for the same reason, while the storm-petrel's tiny egg – it weighs only about 7 grammes – looks no more substantial than a pea. That egg is equivalent to some 25 per cent of the bird's weight. The tystie lays two, sometimes three, eggs and the kittiwake deposits two eggs in its weedy nest-pouch.

Back from the cliff face, where the skylark can make itself heard and the wind strums over croftland and moor, twites are nesting among the heather, wheatears in burrows, whimbrels in shallow scrapes where the heather is short, and the red-necked phalarope selects some marshy spot, training vegetation over its clutch of eggs.

When the young birds hatch, a shuttle service with food begins. In many cases it is a fish stew that the nestlings receive: nourishing fare, delivered beak to beak in the confined spaces. Fulmar chicks are so stuffed with rich food that if alarmed they emulate their parents and spit an oily solution towards the intruder. *Gugas,* the name given to young gannets, means 'fat ones'! Thousands of young birds will die before reaching independence, but seabirds are generally long-lived, and numbers are maintained. The gannets, kittiwakes and fulmars do better than compensating for the year's losses of adult birds; they are so successful that they are at present extending their ranges.

By mid-August, the auks have gone and the young birds – nowhere near full grown – have paddled away from the shore in the twilight. Many kittiwakes have departed, and those that remain utter half-hearted rounds of calling. A dozing fulmar, roused by a strange sound, raises its head, croaks, listens for a few moments, then tucks its beak under a scapular. The young fulmar, bloated with good feeding, makes an effort to preen with its dark bill. It presses a leg against the rim of the nesting area with a webbed foot; it raises itself a little, relaxes, then languidly extends a wing.

A gannet stands protectively over a dark-feathered youngster which has still about its dark plumage a fuzz of white down. The mate arrives. There is a noisy reunion, a scissoring of bills, over the ponderous body of the offspring. The young gannet stirs in its sleep, anticipating yet more food. The last of the young will fly in September. Shearwaters, forsaken by their parents, find their own way to the sea and make the long journey to the wintering areas. One bird covered 4,500 miles, to the east coast of South America, at an average of 250 miles a day. Storm-petrels lose themselves in the wastes of the South Atlantic.

The days shorten. Autumn gales stir the sea, putting more nutrients into circulation. There is a brief second bloom of growth, but now the sun has lost its strength. The northern birds return for the winter. Watchers on Shetland, as summer fades into autumn, see divers in the voes and sounds, sooty shearwaters offshore. Wigeon and tufted duck, with hundreds of long-tailed ducks, breast the shallow sea. Snow-buntings dance on the shore, their calls cutting through the chilling air. Godwit and other waders pack in the Hebridean bays. Pintails have appeared in the Inner Solway; scaup and pochard throng the Firth of Forth. Wild geese make patterns against the grey sky.

The last of the fulmars departs for the open sea, but not for long. Before the Old Year is out, some of them will be back, gliding silently, staring at the cliffs and headlands with their dark Arctic eyes . . .

# 2

# Birdwatch through History

A red-haired boy, one of a school party, came jogging up the path to my Hebridean bothy, and he breathlessly inquired: 'Are ye comin' crakin'?' Half an hour later, in the twilight, the 'craking' was under way. A dozen of us tape-lured the local corncrake to a corner of the meadow, where a mist-net had been set. The bird was captured and examined, had a ring of light alloy slipped over one leg and was released. Such is 'craking'.

On another evening we went 'shearwatering'. In the blackest part of the night, we blundered across slopes on which a goat would feel dizzy, listening for the incoming shearwaters. Each arrival had a torch shone in its face; the beam was held steady as we advanced to collect the disorientated bird, to 'ring and re-lease'. I was shown a shag-hook, used for grasping shags by the neck. It was rather like a shepherd's crook. Any birds recovered were decked with alloy rings and, uninjured but with ruffled plumage and dignity, were allowed to return to their eggs.

Those lads were products of the scientific approach to natural history – to the spirit of an age which demands an explanation for everything. Not one of them sat down and reflected on the grace and beauty of a bird. There was a peak of excitement when I found a dead shark on the beach, and the lads set off with a hammer, intent on knocking out some teeth as grisly souvenirs of their Hebridean adventure.

Times change, and attitudes change with them. The first bird watchers in Scotland had a similar down-to-earth approach. They thought mainly of the good of their stomachs. They ate virtually everything they could catch, as we discover if we examine their middens, near the remains of their old settlements, and find the bones of their prey. Celtic monks, on sea-girt lumps of rock, were at one with nature; some of them wrote poems extolling the beauty of seabirds in their wild settings. The Norsefolk reaped a harvest of seabirds and their eggs. St Kildans became 'bird people' and would have starved without the knack of catching seabirds and storing them for consumption in the winter.

There was a period when 'sportsmen' shot rare birds for fun, or to mount in glass cases as a demonstration of their prowess. Lead pellets cascaded along the ledges being used by auks and kitti-wakes. Shooting birds from a boat at nesting time was a recom-mended diversion. Then men studied 'sea-fowl' scientifically. In due course, there was legal protection for the birds – if you count it as protection when birds are left in peace, and their habitats are grossly polluted.

Who were the first bird-watchers? Doubtless the small parties of humans, venturing northwards in the wake of Pleistocene ice, negotiating forest and bog, living on their wits. They gathered food, hunting and fishing, collecting shellfish on the shore and, as the year waned, plucking fruit and berries. Early Man hit the culinary jackpot when he brought down a red deer or an auroch, for most times the prey item was quite small. From his first appearance in what is now Scotland, some 8,000 years ago, man was a frail figure in the wilderness. He made skin-covered boats and extended his hunting range to the islets and skerries. He slew seals and, doubtless, raided the seabird colonies.

From the prehistoric middens have come the bones of birds: of skua, cormorant, guillemot, gannet, crow. A huntsman on Papa Westray, Orkney, found some great auks and helped the species to oblivion, though it lingered on until the early part of the nineteenth century. Birds and beasts had magical properties. One burial place on an Orcadian island was decked with eagles' talons. When man became more settled, farming developed and cereals were cultivated. Animals were domesticated and bred under controlled conditions. Yet no community could ignore a handy colony of seabirds and their nutritious eggs. Conspicuous birds, like gannets, cormorants and shags, were substantial as well as succulent. (Shags, plucked and dressed, their oil glands removed, are still eaten occasionally. They were retailed in London as Hebridean chickens!)

The monks of the early Church not only watched birds; they wrote about them feelingly. A monk was close to nature – and to God. Nature poems written at this time inspire us still. Stories told of the saints were to be flavoured by medieval fantasy. Who was St Kilda? The sound of this name is rather like the local pronunciation of Hirta, the main island on the archipelago. Who was Ronan, the saint who is associated with Rona? Could he be derived from the Gaelic *'ron'*, meaning seal? We can be more certain of St Baldred, a disciple of St Mungo, who lived with all the austerity of the desert fathers, shivering as he prayed in his cell on the Bass Rock. He doubtless dropped off to sleep to the sound of breaking waves – and the gutteral voices of the gannets. St Columba and his disciples had given lustre to Iona. St Molio (or Molaise) occupied a cell on Holy Isle. St Brendan is credited with the establishment of a monastery on Eileach an Naoimh, one of the Isles of the Sea. St Donnan, settling on Eigg, was slain by the islanders.

St Abbs Head was named after a woman, Ebba, a friend of St Cuthbert. During a visit to nearby Coldingham, he prayed while standing in the sea. It was a night-long vigil, and when he emerged from the water, he was warmed by 'sea otters'. Cuthbert is given credit for founding the first nature reserve, on that sea-fretted group of rocks known as the Farnes. He became specially associated with the eider; the Northumbrians respected him and the bird, it is said, though, as an old fisherman re-marked, the eider is an unpalatable creature, its flesh being tough and fishy! Place-names on the Scottish coast relate to the Papae, a mysterious group of Christian priests – missionaries of the Celtic Church – who served local communities and were influential in the life of Shetland for two centuries or so before the Norsemen arrived.

Research at Jarlshof, near Sumburgh Head, on Shetland, suggests that the Norse folk ate virtually everything they could catch: red-throated diver, gannet, cormorant, shag, the various auks, curlew, gulls, oystercatcher and even the eider. Tearing at such food must have helped to preserve their teeth; this was certainly the case on St Kilda. Among the bones tossed away at Jarlshof were some belonging to Leach's petrel, that mysterious bird of the outer isles. The men of Mingulay were not the only group to clamber about the bird cliffs of Scotland, taking seafowl and their eggs as food, but they are specially remembered because of the awesome setting for their exploits.

The men of Ness, on Lewis, drove their Norse-type boats for over forty miles to the eerie rockscape of Sula Sgeir to collect young gannets, which would be kept for winter consumption.

(The custom has been allowed to continue into the period of bird protection.) It is related that a crew from Ness was wrecked while landing on Sula Sgeir in the middle of last century. They lived for several weeks on bird-flesh and then vanished from the island. The crew of the revenue cutter was alarmed to find the wrecked boat, and an oar standing on end, with a pair of trousers attached to it, but no men. (The marooned crew had been rescued by a homeward-bound Russian ship, which landed them on Rona.)

Tragedies are never forgotten by the folk of the western isles. In 1845, a family living on the Shiant Isles, off Harris, fell to their deaths while seeking birds on the cliffs of Garbh Eilean. Within living memory, islanders were familiar with the taste of seabirds, and a crofter on Eigg, drawing on ancient knowledge, told me how to cook a Manx shearwater. Men did not starve under a gannet-busy sky. In Anglo-Saxon times a poet wrote of the birds nesting on Bass Rock, though not until 1493 was there to be certain documentary evidence of the gannets, always an important food source. Once a gannet had settled for nesting, it could be closely approached without causing alarm. King James IV, visiting the Isle of May in the summer of 1508, would need little stalking skill when he went to 'shut at fowlis with the culveryn'.

In the latter part of the seventeenth century, a young man was hired as a tutor by the Clan MacLeod of the Western Isles; he later acted as land steward, and so he became familiar with a cluster of islands. Martin Martin had a lively, retentive mind. He wrote two books about the Hebrides that are minor classics, packed with illuminating facts and figures. He left us word-pictures of life on St Kilda, which he first visited in 1697, detailing the islander's dependence on birds.

Of the Flannan Isles – which Martin called the Flannin Islands and which seamen commonly referred to as North Hunters – it was recorded that seventy sheep were grazed each summer and that men from Lewis called to 'make a great purchase of fowls, eggs, down, feathers and quills'. They bided their time, watching the weather and promptly turning for home should the east wind turn westerly. Before they began fowling, these superstitious men went to the old chapel of St Flannan, stripped off their upper garments and lay them on a stone near the altar. 'All the crew pray three times before they begin fowling,' wrote Martin. Ancient custom decreed that no fowl should be killed with a stone. 'They account it also unlawful to kill a fowl after Evening Prayers.' In due course, they sailed gleefully for home, their boat laden with 'sheep, fowls, eggs, down, fish, etc'.

Martin did not see the great auk, a giant form of razorbill that was also known as the 'gairfowl'. On St Kilda he talked to men who had observed the bird, and he was thus able to make notes about it. The great auk was gannet-sized, 'of a black colour, red about the Eyes, a large white Spot under each, a long broad bill'. This bird had a stately stance, 'its whole body erected, its Wings short . . .'. The female laid a single egg on bare rock; she did not replace it if it was lost. That egg was reportedly twice the size of a gannet's egg 'and is variously spotted, Black, Green and Dark'.

Martin was told that the great auk appeared on May 1 and departed about the middle of June. He was writing before the change of calendar took place, so his dates are now eleven days out! The very last British specimen perished on St Kilda in 1840, slain by some men who visited Stac an Armin. They surprised the large bird as it slept. Tying its legs together, they kept it for three days, then – the weather deteriorating and the bird plainly the cause of this – they beat it to death with sticks. The great auk, which had paddled its way about the North Atlantic for ages, for it was flightless, was ultimately harried to extinction.

Martin visited St Kilda when this island group was the only British nesting haunt of the fulmar. St Kilda had its own sub-species of wren, and one of the world's great gannetries. The St Kildans supplemented their meagre food supplies – cattle, sheep, potatoes, barley corn – with seabirds and their eggs. Not without reason did Julian Huxley call the islanders 'bird people'. The cull was ritualised; it was also controlled, so that future stocks would be assured. The men operated from small boats and left them to clamber on the cliffs with the verve of goats.

A visitor observed: 'From the period of the arrival of the fowl in the month of March till their departure in November, it is one continued scene of activity and destruction.' Gannet, fulmar and puffin were the main prey species. A stock of dead birds was kept for winter use in drystone structures named cleits. Fulmar oil was used locally and also exported, being kept in the inflated and dried stomachs of gannets. Each fulmar yielded up to half a pint of oil, which on the mainland was used as a medicine. Shops in London and Edinburgh sold it as a remedy for toothache!

Puffins were captured by special dogs, with fowling-rods or by girls who plunged their hands deep into the burrows. The bodies of the puffins were plucked, the carcasses split down the middle to be dried in the open air and consumed by humans, cattle, even the dogs. The first puffin of the season was plucked, though not the wings or tail, and released alive. A custom which seemed barbarous to visitors was nonetheless a vital part of the ritual.

Books have been written about the culture of the 'bird people', which ended when the last of the islanders were taken off St Kilda and re-settled on the mainland in 1930. We leave the subject with some observations by John Macculloch, who visited St Kilda in 1819. 'The air is full of feathered animals,' he wrote. 'The sea is covered with them; the houses are ornamented by them, the ground is speckled with them like a flowery meadow in May. The town is paved with feathers. . . . The inhabitants look as if they had all been tarred and feathered, for their hair is full of feathers and their clothes are covered with feathers.' He added, breathlessly, that 'everything smells of feathers'.

When the Highlands and Isles had become a great sheep-run, shepherds waged a relentless war against birds with hooked beaks, especially the sea eagle. In Sutherland alone, between 1831 and 1834, a total of 171 mature birds was destroyed. The crofters of Shetland took sea eagles, each head earning for the hunter a premium of 3s. 6d., paid by the Commissioners of Supply. On Foula, the bonxies were protected for a time because they harassed the eagles. As firearms improved, men with the money to buy unlimited leisure blasted their way from district to district. Among them was Sir William Milner, who toured Sutherland in 1847, and Charles St John, a specialist in ospreys, who in the summer of 1848 found and destroyed birds near Scourie and Rhiconich.

John Colquhoun varied his sporting life in the 1860s when he developed techniques for shooting sea fowl in the Firth of Forth. He described his exploits with enthusiasm for the benefit of the keen sportsman 'who is just lapsing into the naturalist'. The time to sail was May, when the birds were 'tame' and 'decked in the most imposing and brightest attire'. With his son for company, he sailed from North Berwick in a yawl operated by a man called Kelly, the crew being made up by Kelly's father-in-law and a lad. They used the 'coast slang nicknames' – 'marrots' for guillemots, 'Tommie Nories' for puffins, 'Letter-o-Marques' for cormorants. 'Shoulder duck-guns' were employed against eiders. Landing on the isle of Fidra, our sportsman stalked and shot a drake; he picked off another drake as the yawl sailed down the firth. Now he looked for 'a brown mate' to complete a case of specimens. What was the point of gallantry unless others got to know about it?

Colquhoun frequently missed his quarry, yet found plenty of excuses for this lack of success. Shot dropped round a luckless great northern diver in perfect pattern, but the bird unsportingly made off under water, its body being recovered by a fisherman two days later. The jubilant sportsman recorded that when it was skinned, 'it was discovered that a No.3 pellet had passed through one side of the head and lodged above the eye on the other.' Ugh! Shooting one of a group of three cormorants on The Lamb, he did not recover the body. The same story might be told of the eider duck 'dropped' off Fidra on the following day. He persevered. Another duck, 'hard hit in the body', dived and re-surfaced, when she was 'made safe by a shot. . . . This happy right and left supplied a companion to each of the eider drakes.'

He now needed two species to complete his collection of stuffed specimens of seabirds connected with the Forth. Black guillemot and 'green cormorant' had eluded him. The yawl was hired, despite worsening weather. They sailed to the Isle of May for a black guillemot, the son slaying two gannets *en route*. He actually downed three birds, but one was left 'on the waves'; to tack the boat would have wasted valuable time. The Colquhouns spent the night on the island, leaving the boatmen to keep their craft afloat in stormy conditions. On the following day, Colquhoun junior shot a black guillemot in the 'light speckled plumage of winter'. He then fired at the bird's mate, which 'rose in the air, wheeled, and fell dead in the sea'. So perished the only pair they had seen, and 'we were all . . . proportionately elated.' They returned to the sport of eider-shooting. A case of mounted eiders was presented by Colquhoun to his 'old and very dear friend', one of the ministers of St Cuthbert's church, folklore associating the bird with that saint.

Colquhoun, visiting the Bass, killed a puffin at the first shot, knocked over a razorbill, 'now scarce on the rock', sent pellets singing along the crowded guillemot ledges, bagged two kittiwakes and then shot two purple sandpipers on the shore. Finding the nest of a pair of great black-backed gulls, he tested his theory that the eggs were fresh by taking them to a spring, where they sank like stones. Some herring-gull eggs 'rose up on end, but did not come to the top. We thus saw that they had been sat upon for some time, but not long enough to prevent them from being blown.'

Baird's Shot, 'an inviting snip of rock' that 'juts out upon a line with the walls of the fortress', was the place visited by riflemen who wished to shoot gannets. Woe betide any gannet that settled there. Large, conspicuous and by no means shy, the gannets fell easy prey to generations of sportsmen. There was a year mentioned by Colquhoun when 'the fishermen and others' shot gannets as they flew up the Forth in August 'after an unusually long-continued shoal of herrings'. Consequently, the west side of Bass Rock had been depopulated. The wing pinions of gannets were 'excellent' for making writing-quills. A character named Old Jack obtained a supply for the village teachers.

The Romantics celebrated the profusion of seabirds, in their grand and lonely settings, through prose and verse. Keats enthused about Ailsa Craig: 'Hearken, thou craggy ocean-pyramid! Give answer from thy voice, the seafowl's scream!' To Mendelssohn, Fingal's Cave on Staffa was a 'cathedral of the sea', and so moved was he by its mysterious gloom and flanking basalt columns that he could not describe it, 'only play it', which he did in his *Hebrides Overture*. For every so-called sportsman, who used the Highlands and Islands as a gigantic shooting-gallery, there was a serious-minded observer of wild life – like Harvie-Brown, distilling his knowledge and experiences in *Verebrate Fauna*. The Edmundstons of Buness, in Shetland, gave protection to the few remaining pairs of skuas; they erected a hut on Hermaness Hill and employed a warden. The 'bonxie' was included in the Wild Birds Protection Act of 1880. Ten years later, J. G. Laurenson, with the best of motives, collected some bonxie eggs on Foula and slipped them into the nests of gulls on Noss, to initiate breeding on that island. Bonxies scarcely needed such help, and before long incoming birds were establishing territories on the Hill of Setter.

Richard and Cherry Kearton, who popularised natural history in the late nineteenth century, travelled joyfully in Scotland and were courageous and inventive in their photography of wild birds from 'hides'. Naturalists of today might shudder at some methods used by the Victorians. The Keartons carried a revolver 'for the prosaic and harmless purpose of making a loud report at the top of any cliff in the face of which there is reason for believing some bird's nest, which we desire to photograph, is situated, so that by frightening its owner off we may locate the exact spot at which to make a descent'. Richard dipped a ringed plover egg into a rock pool to ascertain the stage of incubation.

In June 1895, the Keartons sailed for Ailsa Craig and stood amid a swirl of disturbed gannets. Their greatest adventure was a trip to St Kilda in June 1896, in the company of John Mackenzie, who was making his annual visit as factor. They sailed from Glasgow in the *Dunara Castle*. On Hirta, they were approached by women and children who had handkerchiefs full of birds' eggs, mainly those of guillemots and razorbills, for which the charge was a penny each. The brothers stayed in an empty cottage; they were soon aware of being with a bird-people, detecting a strong smell of fulmar oil, 'the plenitude of birds' wings and feathers on the midden heaps, and the number of birds' eggs that adorn nearly every window'.

The St Kildan experience appears to have been for the Keartons what landing on the Galapagos Islands was to Darwin and a sojourn on the Aleutians was to Steller – a revelation of the wonders of nature and of the way a primitive society adapts to the conditions. The experience sustained them for the rest of their lives.

> When we finally left St Kilda on board the *Hebridean*, we were told that the captain intended to steam round by Stack Lee in order to give his passengers a sight of the birds upon it. As the boat came abreast of the towering rock, some members of the crew loaded and ran out a small brass cannon. The tip of a red-hot poker applied to the touch-hole of the gun produced a deafening explosion, which seemed to be instantly flung back at us by Stack Lee, and then thundered and reverberated from crag to crag along the rocky sides of Borrera, sending a great white cloud of startled gannets into the air above us.

Nothing was too insignificant to be photographed. They pictured the local type of horsehair rope, a puffin gin, the eggs of the St Kilda wren – compared with the eggs of the mainland wren, and the St Kilda 'mailboat', which was a hollowed-out piece of wood attached to a bladder made from a sheep's skin. Noticing the St Kildans' dexterity on the crags, the brothers photographed the ankle of a St Kildan male alongside one of Richard's ankles! These Keatons, who had been born and reared among the sheep-farmers of the Pennine dales, were able to identify themselves with local people to the extent that Richard spent a vigil with a gun, his 'hide' a cleit, his bait some fish offal, to shoot predatory birds such as the hooded crow, for which the St Kildans had 'no time'. A crow was shot. 'After I had picked up my trophy, and prepared him for the skinning-knife, I re-entered my place of hiding; but to small purpose, as the old maid's cats living next door to us scented my offal, and by their assiduous attentions made it impossible for me to get another shot.'

Such whimsical happenings should not divert attention from the brothers' main concern: the varied bird life. Richard considered that the greatest ornithological sight 'is the prodigious flock of puffins on Soa'. They visited the island, watched the puffin gin being used and marvelled at the profusion of birds.

> Puffins simply swarmed in the air above it, on the rocks and earth of which it is composed, and dotted the sea all round as far as the powers of a pair of good field-glasses could make them out. Those on the wing twirled round and round in a great cloud that perceptibly interfered with the light of day as it passed over us. The swish of their wings made a continuous buzz, and a stone thrown across the path of their flight could not have failed to bring down one or more victims. The whole scene simply beggared description, and the parasites that fell off the birds as they flew over us swarmed on our caps and jackets, a few of them finding more succulent quarters, much to our discomfort and annoyance.

It was their first encounter with fulmars – and, of course, they were squirted when they went too close to a sitting bird. 'The oil gives off such a strong odour that everything in St Kilda smells of it. I fetched two fowling-rods away with me as curiosities, but when I got them home discovered that they could not be tolerated anywhere in the house. They were, therefore, relegated to an exposed corner in the garden, and remained there bleaching from June to November, at the end of which time the smell appeared to have quite gone, and I took them indoors. In a few days, however, it returned again with something akin to its former strength.'

Shetland lured the Kearton brothers, and a photograph published in 1898 shows Cherry, with camera, advancing on a guano-encrusted ledge, intent on photographing a shag. They made a 'turf hovel' to come to close quarters with a pair of Arctic skuas. A bird returned to the nest but was uneasy, being upset by the glint of the camera lens 'peeping from beneath a shaggy eyebrow of heather on the side of the artificial howe'. Twite nested in a Shetland garden, using 'a straggling young honeysuckle plant tied back to the stone wall surrounding the enclosure'. The weather being wet and windy, the brothers suspended a rhubarb leaf over the nest to shelter the sitting bird! Schoolboys were recruited to 'drive' red-necked phalarope to 'within my field of focus'.

Nonetheless, the brothers had the welfare of birds at heart. They were distressed on Ailsa Craig when they saw visitors stoning seabirds. A guillemot was struck. 'She rolled off the ledge and went twirling – a disordered bundle of feathers – down, down, hundreds of feet into the sea below. This made my blood boil with indignation, and I lashed out in language which was very much more forcible than polite.' On Ailsa, the puffins were 'feathered persecutors'. They drove the rabbits from their burrows. 'Several times whilst seated on a boulder, making observations after the light of day had grown too weak for photographic purposes, I was suddenly startled by the piercing scream of a distressed rabbit ringing out in the still evening air. . . .'

Frances Pitt, a conservationist at heart, before conservation became the vogue, wrote after a visit to Shetland: 'If people must collect, let them stick to postage stamps [a pretty thought!] and leave the wild things of our remote wild spots to rear their chicks and live out their little lives in peace.' She attempted to photograph the black guillemots in Lerwick harbour, 'but again and again we were defeated by the elusive "tystie". . . . The bird invariably dived just as we were getting within range, only to come up again many yards away.'

Visitors to Shetland today see the futuristic installations and the 'everlasting flame' of the oil terminal at Sullom Voe. These have brought a degree of prosperity to the north, but many conservationists shudder at the consequences of a major oil-spill.

When the fuel tank of a visiting ship was ruptured during berthing operations, over 1,000 tons of heavy oil entered the sea, much of it spreading with rainbow hues into Yell Sound. In the black scum that appeared on the tideline were dead birds: over 100 great northern divers, almost 300 long-tailed duck, over 500 eiders and 600 tysties. The once-despised sand-eel is now being sought by some Shetland boats; the catch is processed into fishmeal for export. Yet sand-eels are a major food item for auks and terns.

Man, on his first appearance in Scotland, was among the frailest of the creatures. He now has an awesome measure of control over the natural scene, the birds and the beasts.

# 3

# Lochailort: On the Road to the Isles

I have seen the Road to the Isles, between Fort William and Mallaig, develop from a superior cart-track, with grass up the middle, to an ample highway, though it still plays hide-and-seek with the Mallaig railway line. At the Loch Eil pass, hillsides were blasted away to admit a length of new road. Towards Arisaig, this highway to the sea retains something of its old character, and around any one of the bends a Mallaig fish lorry could be lurking, ready to pounce!

The Road to the Isles was, to me, just that – a road to be followed, at the best possible speed, so that I might catch the boat for the Small Isles. The old 'island fever' rose with every passing mile, and I would render Kenneth Macleod's famous marching song with only the hooded crows, the ravens and the red deer to hear me. When I was soaked to the skin, forced to drape my outer clothes before the kitchen range of a Highland hotel, I added 'Loch Aga' to the list.

No bird-watching opportunities were missed, of course. There would be eiders by Loch Linnhe, a buzzard around the mouth of Glenfinnan and a red-throated diver cruising on Loch Eil. At Eastertime I might see a great northern diver on Lochailort and hear once again of the possibility of a pair of these majestic birds having nested on a lochan in the district. Later in the year, the cuckoo's call floated across the glens, and I remember one wretched bird, cuckooing from a fencing post in a 'wee shower' with a bead of water at the tip of its bill. Herons stood like grey posts on the shore of Loch nan Uamh. Frenzied oystercatchers dashed about the white sands near Arisaig. *En route*, in the half light, I might see ragged bands of red deer, the antlers of the stags cast, the winter hair falling away in tufts.

A herring-gull convention was usually in progress at Mallaig. Rooftops near the harbour were convenient perches. Every ship's mast, every gable end, had its feathered totem. A gull would utter a peevish *kyow,* and other birds come in on the act. A dozen laughing cries would ring across the Sound of Sleat. The bright eyes of innumerable gulls scanned the fishing-boats as they fidgeted at their moorings or came sweeping in from the sea with foam at their bows. The herring-gull is a bird tuned to the rush and bustle of the twentieth century – a bird not too large, not too small; an opportunist bird, catholic in its diet, as interested in a discarded crust of bread as in any fish that fell on to the jetty. Once I saw an accidental spillage of herring, a flurry of grey and white feathers, gulls emerging from the scrum with fish-tails protruding from their bills, breathlessly gobbling down the food before other birds could filch it. If any bird knows the miseries of indigestion, it must be a Mallaig herring-gull!

The Road to the Isles is a Road of Romance. Every mile has its reminders of Bonnie Prince Charlie, who sailed away from the shore of Loch nan Uamh when his cause was lost. I paid homage to the petrified Highlander on the monument at Glenfinnan and found one of the Prince's hidey-holes, a shallow cave in an enchanted, moss-lagged stretch of woodland high above Glen Meoble, where, to judge by the litter, he must have been inordinately fond of canned ale.

Deciding, in early April, to follow the Road but to stop short of Mallaig – to ignore my beloved Small Isles – I based myself on Lochailort. It was officially spring. Mild air had swept the glens, stimulating a flush of new growth on the best land. Green tassels bedecked the larches. The spearpoints of iris jutted in dense masses from tracts of marshy ground. Spring had yet to storm the hills, and to walk a few yards uphill was to stride back into winter. Here was a sodden carpet of deadness – a wilderness tinted cream, fawn, orange and brown. On the night before I arrived at the hotel, some red stags had visited the dustbins. In high places, the bedraggled, tick-ridden beasties stared at me hard and long, as though undecided whether to 'freeze' or use up energy – and food reserves – by trotting away.

A few small birds did their best to enliven the landscape. There was a cock wheatear, singing its short, cheerful, sometimes wheezy little refrain. The aria of a willow-warbler came from a bird perched on a rowan that hung over a hillside burn. Squatting on its nest in an isolated thorn – a nest lined with sheep's wool –

was a 'grey crow', the celebrated 'whoodie', a north-western variant of the carrion crow, identical but for its grey jumper. The honk of a crow may be the only sound to break the winter stillness in the Highlands, and like the herring-gull this bird is catholic in its tastes. One moment it feasts on the remains of a deer; the next it is collecting shellfish on the shore, dropping them on the rocks to shatter the shells. In spring, the hooded crow haunts the lambing fields, gorging itself on afterbirth and also causing fearful damage to any weak or ailing lambs.

On Loch Ailort, the eiders were courting. Drakes called *ah-oo-ah*, a sound which a friend compares to that made by a duchess who has just had her bottom pinched! Eiders in flight settled naturally into a 'line ahead' formation, keeping low. I was usually too far from the birds to see the drake's pastel tones – the delicate pink on the breast, the green on the nape – and from a distance the ducks looked dowdy by comparison. Eiders picked shellfish from the floating cages connected with the fish-farm. In spring, the drake eider ensures that the duck has a time of uninterrupted feeding, to build up condition against the time of egg-laying and the period of incubation. The drake would mate – and depart. The duck would establish a nest, lag it with down plucked from her breast and sit with hormone-induced patience. The duck would then have to marshal the black young birds for a walk to the sea, during which they would almost certainly be harassed by gulls.

During a vigil at twilight, I heard three grunts and a squeak: the sounds made by a roding woodcock, which passed by some fifty feet above the tousled ground near a pinewood. The bird maintained a precise height. I waited. The bird returned, uttering that distinctive soft croaking, followed by the sneeze-like *tsiwick*. The sitting bird hopes to escape detection by its immobility and cryptic colouration. I once met a Highland stalker who claimed he could detect a sitting woodcock by the sparkle in its eyes! After I had been chatting with him one day, he nudged me, pointing to the ground a few yards away, and I saw a woodcock sitting amid the wizened leaves. That clutch of eggs hatched in the early morning; the downy mites that emerged were balls of russet and ochraceous-buff, standing on lead-grey legs. An adult woodcock, ten yards away, slowly beat its wings and croaked to distract my attention from the chicks.

It was the time of year when the sky tones were often darker than those of the hilltops. A day might begin cloudy and wet, with the obligatory 'wee shower' lasting an hour or two, but by evening the clouds had dispersed. Hard, clear northern sunlight probed the district like a searchlight beam. The northerly wind moderated. Grey geese were on the move, from the 'tatie' fields of Perth towards their far northern nesting grounds.

A pair of goosanders flew under one of the arches of Glenfinnan's concrete viaduct, and their rakish bodies were dwarfed by a mass of concrete. A buzzard's call – *pee-oo* – drifted through the moist air. On my march up the glen I carried a cromack, as recommended by Kenneth MacLeod in his *Road to the Isles*. My stick was not of the Highland variety; there was no true handle, just a section of deer horn, hollowed, to be used as a whistle. (Before the day was out, it would whistle in the wind!) I was overtaken by a cigarette-smoking walker who was out to humble some Munros. Red deer moved across a landscape seeking fresh vegetation and being prevented by wire netting from entering an area of young coniferous trees. In the rides, the grass was hock-high; on the hill the deer looked for strands of greenstuff on a prairie of tousled growth. Other deer lay on the ridges, waiting for the friendly night, when they might descend without being detected to the edge of the burn. Five hinds emerged from behind a screen of birks and began to fill their bellies with stuff that resembled straw.

My path began to climb; the burn was deep-sunk in a gorge that was overhung by rowans and birches. Several meadow pipits fluttered ahead of me. A golden eagle trimmed its wings and tail to the air currents around Stob Core nan Cearc. The bird slipped out of sight, then reappeared in a powerful upward glide, cruising towards The Streap. In a matter of minutes it was a black spot against the blue arc of the sky. In winter, the eagle depends on carrion for almost half its diet. It descends on the corpses of deer and sheep, feeding so rapaciously it may be temporarily incapable of flight. A ghillie told me of the bloated eagle that attempted to escape from him – on foot!

I climbed to the sub-Arctic world of the 'tops', measuring my progress by the number of times I paused to rest. Patches of snow appeared to view. The stagshorn became common. Tatters of mist went by, and through a rent in mist I saw grey cliffs, the cores of ancient drifts, and a party of red deer, stags and hinds together. Now the rocks were sheathed by ice, and the plants were of the type that puts down long roots and keeps its head low for fear of being decapitated by the cruel wind. I crossed the ridge, slipped into the lee of crags – and was transfixed by the view ahead. Here was a skyline worthy of the Alps, with snow-capped hills beyond snowless ridges, like pearl-white teeth set on a gum of brown. Ben Nevis held the central position. On the previous day, visitors to the Ben were being warned of the danger of avalanches.

Snow squeaked under my feet. Three ptarmigan – our Arctic grouse – left the edge of a snowfield with no preparatory run: the effect was explosive. The wind tickled their tails as they departed at speed, following the contours of the hilltops, matching the snowfields because they were clad in their winter-white plumage. It was no surprise to see ptarmigan on these exposed ridges, for the wind disperses the snow, revealing coarse plant food: blaeberry, crowberry, heather. Ptarmigan prefer to run rather than fly, for their white wings may alert an eagle.

On a 'damply' dawn, the following day, I visited a glen where the coarse vegetation in a limited area had been trodden down until it resembled coconut matting. This was a *lek*, an assembly ground for amorous black grouse. When the greyhens are looking for mates, they visit this display ground and naturally head for the finest birds. The mating order among blackcocks is established by display rather than battle; it is a triumph of guile over brute force. Two cocks face each other, drooping their wings, fanning their under-tail coverts, crooning and hissing. Large, blue-black bodies contrast with the yellows and fawns of dead vegetation. The hissing is explosive, not quite a sneeze. You could match it by suddenly removing a tyre-valve from your bicycle. When mating has taken place, the greyhens depart. Like the eider ducks, they go through the remainder of the breeding season without masculine involvement.

Loch Eil held a mirror-reflection of the russet hills. A blob of white on the water represented a wee bothy standing on a remote stretch for the far shore. Promontories and islets, with their sentinel pines, were faithfully represented, the demarcation line between land and water being lost in the blackness of deep shadow. Ripples led my eyes to where a pair of red-throated divers swam low in the water, their brown backs almost awash.

Red eyes, like rubies, were set in pale grey heads. The rust-red throat patches of these strange birds appeared to glow in sunlight. The redthroats swam with their heads well up, beaks tilted, as though wearing tight clothes. That rusty throat patch was clear to see.

Time would tell if the birds used Loch Eil for nesting. Redthroats commute to the coast when they are hungry and can make do with quite small stretches of water. A quacking *kok-ok-ok* marks the aerial progress twixt nest and sea. A bird must alight and take off from water but has perfected the skill of using limited space, with the result that a lochan of modest size on the hill can be used for nesting. I recall the merest lochan on Rhum from which a redthroat rises with a flurry of wings, only to switch off its motor and glide – sometimes for a mile or so – to alight on the sea far below. Sandy bays on the north-west coast of Scotland are clear enough for a visitor to see the divers swimming underwater, questing for fish. Yet divers have a poor breeding record. A disturbed bird is reticent to return to the nest; half an hour may go by before it covers its eggs again, and meanwhile those eggs run the risk of being filched by the gulls. Failed breeders, which pass the daylight hours preening and sleeping, are a familiar sight. I was to see up to six redthroats on one stretch of water in mid-June.

The banshee-wail of a diver at its nesting area can stop a naturalist in his tracks with excitement and can chill the blood of anyone who is unfamiliar with the species. The birds on Loch Eil swam silently together. Good weather might be expected. Martin Martin – he who wrote of the birds on St Kilda – described the diver as the 'rain goose'; it was larger than a duck, and 'makes a doleful noise before a great rain'. The sleek and colourful nuptial plumage is in striking contrast with the pale winter garb of birds loitering in groups on a sea of gun-metal grey.

I watched a second pair of divers arrive on Loch Eil. The birds pitched down some 150 yards from those already in occupation. It was a tense moment, leading to much dipping of bills in water, followed by shallow dives, as the first pair became excited and set about releasing some surplus nervous energy. When the two pairs became reconciled to each other's presence, I looked around. There was a large stag on the skyline. Hooded crows called huskily after a departing raven.

Slop, slop, peat and sphagnum; burns and bogs; wet stones, moss and lichen – this was the sort of terrain in which I walked. Sheltering in a bothy at the head of Glen Pean as raindrops bounced on the roof, I heard the sharp calling of a dipper and the raven's doleful *pruk*. From the doorway I watched a peregrine falcon pass: light, lithesome, flashing through the damp air on scimitar-shaped wings.

I was invariably sodden when I returned to the hotel, and the bathwater soon acquired a peat-brown tint. In the evening I could meet the local people, emerging bleary-eyed from their long Highland winter. There were some hard drinkers among them. One told me that he drank whisky as a medicine; another said he was scared to open his eyes, in case he bled to death! An in-comer, becoming lyrical, poured a few 'wee drammies' down his throat and described his favourite view, with its 'whisky-toned pools', its 'gin-clear sea' and islands that were 'sherry-hued'!

My favourite view of land and water is from a point near Arisaig, where the dark rocks and expanses of weathered quart-zite give way to a jade sea that stretches away to the islands: to Eigg, merging with Rhum. The distinctive profile of Eigg reminds me of a gigantic aircraft-carrier, and Rhum is a fantasy of abruptly soaring hills (for which the local name is 'coolins'). I beheld them as the sun dipped. When it was tickling the horizon, the islands were like black cut-outs propped at the rim of the sea.

The air lanes held the Vs of departing grey geese. A skein of sixty birds flew over Loch Morar, below the level of the hills, and swept grandly over the Sound of Sleat, close to Eigg. They remained low but occasionally broke the skyline, when they were like a string of dark beads hanging from cloud to cloud. From Bracaria, on the shore of Loch Morar, I followed a path across an assembly of hillocks – part of the Rough Bounds – to the shore of Loch Nevis, a remote area indeed. Flocks of meadow pipits animated the peat-and-heather wilderness. A lark produced a cascade of song, and I roused a young red stag from its bed in a hollow. It was the time of lambing. At a croft beside Loch Nevis, the contralto calls of the ewes mingled with the soprano arias of new lambs. I was on the edge of a cloud mass, with clear sky and blue water to the west. The big bens of the hinterland were wrapped in cloud and mist.

I slogged back up the hill, pausing to look at Sgor na Ciche, a most shapely hill. Spurning the main path, I followed a ridge high above Morar and then tried to find a satisfactory route to the path by the loch. Walking became mountaineering. Under the gaze of two startled ravens, I descended some thousand feet in about twenty minutes, crag-hopping, slithering on scree, bounding from one patch of turf to another, clambering over boulders. The ravens chattered to each other about the erratic behaviour of *homo sapiens*. A black-throated diver looked – and dived.

During the night, I awoke and rubbed an itch that had developed on my left leg. The itching intensified. I groaned. During my walk to Nevis, a tick had climbed aboard for a ride and also to drink my blood. Here was the dreaded Black Spot o' the Heilands! There was more itching, from high on my back. The skill is to identify ticks before they settle down, or to get them to release their hold by tickling their tails with the glowing end of a cigarette, risking third-degree burns. Otherwise, the mite, having buried its head in your flesh, swells up like a wee black grape as it drinks. I visited the local equivalent of the African witch-doctor, and 'spirit' was advised. 'Och, something like turpentine.' I settled for Dettol and recalled when, on the Small Isles, everyone was using after-shave lotion to combat insect bites.

I thumbed a lift on a lobster-boat and was put ashore on a beach of silver sand near the point of Ardnish, sharing this peninsula with the ghosts of a lost community. The fisherman dawdled during the voyage, his boat cruising near the islets of Loch nan Uamh, which were decked with herring and great black-backed gulls. The water became bumpy, and the skipper's collie dog was agitated. There was 'nothing between us and America except open water', he said. The dog whined. A passing raven prompted a discussion on whether or not this was a good or a bad omen. A tystie dived. Shags leapt from their nesting islets and made an untidy job of landing on the loch. We rounded the point into calmer water.

When the boat had moved off in a haze of exhaust fumes, I was left on a tract of ground speckled with primroses. There was a sad air about the groups of roofless buildings I passed. Droppings and slots testified to recent visits by red deer, and everywhere I saw the fleshy spears of flag iris. The dwellings of the largest settlement occupied a raised beach, with a sea view in front and a sweep of lazybeds behind. I sought out the M1 of Ardnish: a paved path between birches, then between ash and oak and finally across open ground, in the company of buzzards and ravens. Squared slabs of gabbro, with ditching on either side where this was possible, provided a durable all-weather route to the outer world. I ate a packed lunch at a high point, from which Eigg and Rhum could be seen, presiding over a turquoise sea.

Next morning, there was just enough blue in the sky to 'patch a Dutchman's breeks'. At the hostelry, there was talk about cormorants – more precisely how to cook cormorants. A local man once announced that he was holding a wine and cormorant-tasting party. Nobody turned up!

# 4

# Canna: Nights are for Shearwaters

By the end of May, the Hebridean days are endless. I sailed to the Small Isles, south of Skye, where – with a high-pressure system lodged over Scotland – night was a murky interlude between two long days. I voyaged in a misty world. The land lacked substance, being represented by blotches of blue and grey. A low-flying cormorant admired its reflection in the sea. A gannet crossed an otherwise empty sky. The white of the gannet is that of the detergent advertisement; this bird was not only solitary but silent, free for the moment from the hubbub of the gannetry: from the grating calls, *gurruk, gurruk, gurruk*, the bowing and scraping, the clashing of spear-like bills.

My first crossing from Mallaig to the Small Isles had been on the *Western Isles*, captained by Brucie Watts. 'It's going to be rough,' someone said. 'Brucie's got his cap on!' No one knew these waters better than Brucie, who had a cheerful disregard for the fury of wind and water. One February dawn, when a gale was strumming the telephone wires beside the harbour at Mallaig, and even the gulls were grounded, he looked into the blackest part of the sky and remarked: 'Och! but it's clearing!'

Then there was Willie Callendar, who captained the Mac-Brayne ship, the *Loch Arkaig*. Willie claimed that gulls were the reincarnation of seamen, their ranks indicated by stripes on the wings. He was doubtless thinking of immature gulls. One day, as I chatted with him, a former lieutenant-commander flew by! The old *Arkaig*, of 179 tons, was originally a minesweeper and had a wooden hull. There was no hold for goods, and livestock was borne to the isles in crates. Passengers and goods thus formed an uneasy relationship, and I recall a Ministry vet, on a regular inspection tour of the islands, settling down to sleep on a heap of rope and canvas. Both Brucie and Willie are dead. On my voyage to Canna, I studied every passing gull, looking for two that might have the rank of captain. Then a group of shearwaters slid into view; these pigeon-sized birds with narrow wings were using the updraught of the waves to move without the energy-consuming process of wing-beating.

Sunlight burned its way through the mist on the section between Rhum and Canna. The day became bright and hot. Our boat slipped between Canna and its satellite, the isle of Sanday, with the ponderous form of a Catholic church, built in a time of religious certainty, rising like a Gothic watchtower above the Sanday shore. We nosed into the jetty; the boat's propellers stopped and went into reverse; a tystie dived through a mass of air bubbles. We were welcomed by an islander, his tractor, trailer – and wee dog. Deciding to ring up home, I visited the blue-painted telephone kiosk, the door of which sagged on its hinges, witnessing to the savage nature of the Hebridean wind. It amused me to hear the crooning of eiders blending with the telephone's dialling tone. Several eiders swam on a high tide, within 25 yards of the box.

Canna has that satisfying island 'feel', with more than a hint of remoteness. It lies about halfway between Mallaig and South Uist, orientated east and west, cresting at 690 feet. The northern cliffs deflect the wind that arrives from the coldest quarter, sheltering the main habitations and the best farm land, which is set out on terraces of basalt, derived from the coarse ash and dust spewed out by ancient volcanoes. Canna, an island of fertile soil, has long been famed for producing potatoes in May. Canna House, presiding over its little estate, keeps an eye on Sanday, which is a crofters' island. Compass Hill, on Canna, plays games with compass needles. A tower on an isolated pillar was compared by Walter Scott with a falcon's nest that 'o'erhangs the bay'. Climbing the rock was dangerous 'to aught but goat or mountain deer'.

Having visited Canna in spring, with the sky a cloudless blue, I tend to think of it as a sunny island. Yet the parish minister in 1794 wrote: 'The air is generally moist, and the weather rainy. The southerly and easterly winds, which are the most frequent, are almost constantly attended with rain. . . .' Walter Scott, touring the Northern Lights in 1814, remembered the Hebridean seas for their turbulence. 'The wind shifted and became squally. The mingled and confused tides that run among the Hebrides got us among their eddies and gave the cutter such concussions that, besides reeling at every wave, she trembled from head to stern with a sort of very uncomfortable and ominous vibration.' And this was during the Scottish summer!

Sanday is tethered to Canna by a footbridge, and my bothy lay near that bridge. The curious name Canna may be derived from a Gaelic word, *cana*, meaning 'porpoise'. Or it could be 'isle of rabbits'! Sanday is the straightforward 'sand isle'. Canna, a happy island, was transferred to the care of the National Trust for Scotland in 1981 by Dr John Lorne Campbell, who continues to live at Canna House and runs a farm noted for its Highland cattle and Cheviot sheep.

I sauntered forth to explore the western side of Sanday, walking through a garden that was a riot of spring growth, including marsh marigolds; pausing beyond the bridge to look at a wayside shrine with its stained glass that would be brought to sparkling, colourful life as the sun set, and watching ringed plover go through their distraction rituals on the beach. When they were not flirting their wings, the birds ran so quickly and smoothly they might have been fitted with castors. A snipe reluctantly left a nest containing four eggs. Eight ravens launched themselves from a cliff overlooking the sea. A fulmar passed, silently, fixing its dark eyes on me. From Canna came the cuckoo's doleful aria, followed by the husky double notes of a corncrake.

The setting sun spread watercolour tints across sky and sea. As the islands darkened, a buzzard mewed. And, of course, the eiders crooned. At midnight, I walked beside the sea, *en route* for the grassy slopes on which the shearwaters were nesting. The approach was much easier than I found on Rhum, where the birds nest high on the coolins. Up there, in snow and mist, the shearwaters have transformed their nesting haunts. The birds' droppings enriched the ground, stimulating a rich growth of grass, which is grazed by the deer. The result is a collection of 'lawns' in an area where you would expect nothing more than a few impoverished plants.

Canna offered me an approach on level ground. The night was humid, and in the gloom I watched a buzzard glide by, as mysterious as a bat. Buzzards are among the predators at a shearwater colony: one reason why the oceanic birds return to land at dead of night. My final approach was over steep ground, which is a boon to birds that are graceful in flight, awkward on land. In the air, shearwaters glide and twist, kept buoyant by the uprushing wind, their long wings cutting cleanly through the air. The birds turn one way, then the other, first revealing the dark upperparts, then the white of underbody and wing. So they cruise up to 200 miles from their nests, their quick eyes locating fish shoals that are near the surface. Groups of shearwaters, silently rising, falling, circling, perform an aerial ballet between the islands.

It is quite different on land. The birds pitch down with a succession of thuds, and they shuffle about on their bodies. How do they find their nests in the darkness? They have a strong musky odour; maybe they can locate their own burrows by smell. It does not explain how dozens, if not hundreds, of shearwaters fly around in darkness without colliding.

I sat on the rim of the hill, with the nearest shearwater burrow no more than five yards away. When the Rhum birds first return from their ocean wanderings, they may have to clear away snow before they can enter the old burrows. A pair loiters in a burrow and has a brief 'honeymoon' period at sea, where the birds feed without interruption, building up their reserves of fat against the protracted rigours of the nesting season. The egg will be incubated for over a month. The chick, initially covered with pale-grey down, is so well catered for that eventually it weighs more than the adult, at which stage it is deserted, left to make its own way to the sea.

The night sky was not truly dark; it was faintly illuminated by the loom of the Heiskeir light, seven miles to the south-west. (On this remote islet the Canna cattle were grazed in summer.) *Cock-a-row, cock-a-row*: a shearwater shattered the stillness, and for the first time that night I felt chilled. I expected a rush of birds, for some thousand pairs nest on Canna. Instead, there could have been a dozen in flickering flight against the black mass of the hill. I switched on a torch, hearing a faint sound five yards away. The powerful beam revealed a dazzled, temporarily disorientated bird, which was soaking up the bright directional light like a prima donna at the opera. On another night, hundreds of shearwaters would be in flight, their cries merging into a strange wavering sound, one moment intense, another moment faint, only to break out again into an eerie chorus.

Next morning, traversing a deserted hill slope, I found a few feathers and one mangled shearwater wing to hint at the nature of the burrows. A visiting ornithologist removed a plug of turf, fumbled in the dark passage beyond and withdrew a bemused shearwater. The nictitating membranes passed over its eyes as it was suddenly exposed to the fierce light of day. The eyes were revealed again, like tiny jewels. I saw the shearwater's intricate bill, with its bevelled nostrils and a terminal hook. Here was the gurgling, cackling demon of the Hebridean night, staring at me from a head as black as soot. The bird-watcher fixed a light alloy ring round a leg and slipped the shearwater into the burrow. He had already 'ringed' the bird's mate. In normal circumstances, the egg of a shearwater does not have daylight directly on it, and so cryptic colouration is not necessary. My brief glance at the egg revealed it to be white, oval in shape.

I toured the island of Sanday, initially with the company of four grey seals. I followed the path along the shore to the crofting houses. One old crofter, his face tanned like mahogany, wore a woolly hat, a pullover and some old trousers, which were tucked into wellingtons. His old mack was tied by string. There was no concession, in this ample workaday wear, to the coming of spring. On the cliff, fulmars had settled among the sea pinks, and the birds looked benign. A cuckoo, in the absence of trees, perched on the summit of a low crag and rendered its monotonous double-note call. I wandered into an area colonized by herring-gulls, some of which shouted from aloft, while others stood at their nests and 'jabbered', fixing me with their fierce-looking yellow eyes. More gulls were nesting on a stack, which I approached down a gully clogged with driftwood, including telegraph poles. Above an open beach, an oystercatcher harried a hooded crow so persistently that it collided with the larger bird.

At low tide, that beach was an unsightly expanse of dark boulders, festooned with weed, littered with driftwood, which an old lady was patiently collecting as firewood. While giving her a hand, I saw a herring-gull nest in a most picturesque setting. Isolated ridges extended above the splash-mark of the tides. Grey rock was adorned by patches of yellow lichen and cushions of thrift. The nest – and there was only one nest – was a grass-lined scrape between the patches of pink and expanses of lichen that had the colour of iodine – a joyous sight in a black environment.

I awoke each morning a little before 7 a.m. and listened for the crooning of eider drakes. After a bath and breakfast, I usually sat in the sunshine at a point overlooking the sound, which was silvered by the strong light. Those were moments to cherish. I became familiar with the appearance of some of the Cheviot sheep and their podgy lambs. I nicknamed one of the beef cattle Gormless. Having contrived to get an old basket over its horns, it took five minutes to free itself – and then walked off with yards of briar clinging to its shaggy tail!

I climbed to the 'attic' of Canna – to a tract of moorland bearing a thousand orchid spikes – passing from the sounds of the shore (the creaking calls of terns, piping of oystercatchers) to where the day was punctuated by the sad little whistle of a golden plover. It was a day of such clarity that The Long Island appeared as a line of blue hummocks and the cuillins of Skye were sharp and clear at 20 miles. I located the Neise Point lighthouse on Skye, at over 30 miles, and then picked out what must have been Harris, at 60 miles. As if that were not enough, I found myself at the edge of cliffs some 600 feet high. Grassy areas are frequented by wild goats. Grey seals pup near Garrisdale. Shags nest on low ledges by the sea.

I collected a souvenir – a feather so large I could use it as a fan. It had been moulted by an immature sea eagle. I looked around until my eyes prickled with fatigue, but the erstwhile owner of that feather was not to be seen. Perhaps it had settled on some quiet crag, contemplating whatever crosses the mind of an eagle, looking around with quick, bright eyes on a jumbled cliffscape beside a sparkling sea.

For a really close view of a sea eagle, I would have to go to Rhum . . .

Dunnet Head, in Caithness, the northernmost point on the British mainland. The lighthouse, a squat structure on cliffs some 300 feet high, directs its beams across the turbulent Pentland Firth

The *Loch Arkaig,* of fond memory, swings into Loch Scresort, island of Rhum, as part of its regular service between the Small Isles

A third-year sea eagle, photographed on the island of Rhum, where the Nature Conservancy Council tends young birds brought from Norway in the hope that this impressive species, exterminated by shepherds and sportsmen, will re-establish itself as a British breeder

A Manx shearwater at its nesting burrow on one of the Rhum coolins

Ullapool, by Loch Broom, sprang into prominence during the herring boom. There is a car ferry from here to Stornoway

A party of bird-watchers is put ashore on Handa, an island off Sutherland which holds one of the most impressive gatherings of seabirds in Britain

*(Above)* Old Man of Hoy, a 450-foot-high stack which stands with the dramatic emphasis of an exclamation mark off the west coast of the island of Hoy, second largest of the Orkney group. At nearby St John's Head, the cliffs soar vertically to an elevation of over 1,000 feet. This coast resounds with the voices of seabirds

*(Left)* The Isle of Noss, Shetland, has a profusion of seabirds. Gannets nest on broad ledges on and around the Noup. The highest cliffs face eastwards, over a sea abounding with herring and mackerel, to catch which the gannets plunge-dive, descending to the water like white meteorites

*(Above left)* A great black-backed gull returns to its nest to shelter new-hatched chicks from the glare of the summer sun. Its large size and deep voice readily distinguish it from other species of gull

*(Above)* The bridled form of the common guillemot. There is a proportion of such birds in most colonies, and the number increases the further north one travels. Dense throngs of guillemots are found on many Scottish sea cliffs and stacks

*(Left)* A cormorant stands guard over its downy young on a Scottish island. The stance is virtually upright, for the short and powerful legs and webbed feet — the propulsion unit when the bird is underwater — are set well back on the body

Watchers on the cliffs, Isle of Noss, with a row of nesting fulmars on a ledge a few yards away

A section of the gannetry, as seen by the visitor who looks over the cliff edge. The gannets build 'drum' nests, like miniature volcanoes

A puffin stands beside its nesting burrow on Noss. A bird which spends eight months of the year at sea never looks completely happy when on land

A group of puffins idling away the summer afternoon

*(Above)* Fulmars and sea pinks. Shetland has become one gigantic fulmar colony, and birds are tending to spend longer on land than was the case a few years ago. Other petrels nesting in Britain fly in from the sea, at the changeover in nesting duty, only during the darkest part of the night

*(Left)* An Arctic tern, with red bill and black crown, alights at its nest, holding its long wings aloft momentarily before tucking them away. The bird winters among the ice floes of Antarctica

# 5

# Isle of Rhum:
# Eagles and Sheep-ticks

I awoke on Rhum to hear a steady hissing sound – a 'wee shower' that was to last half a day. With an oceanic climate, and coolins sticking up like giant bell tents, a high rainfall is assured. On Rhum, I have seriously entertained the thought that human beings might suffer from rust. Mercifully, I arrived before the onset of the midge season. Midges fly in dense brown clouds, and there is no defence against them save a rapid retreat into the hoose. Should you kill a midge on Rhum, then a thousand others will come to the funeral. E. M. Nicholson, when he was Director-General of the Nature Conservancy (an organisation that acquired the island in 1957) wrote: 'Non-scientific visitors are often most impressed by the numbers and viciousness of the horse flies or clegs, the midges and the sheep-ticks.'

Edwin Waugh, the Lancashire dialect writer, was familiar with the 'stinging insects' of Rhum, and he wrote that their vindictiveness was something startling. 'They came down in murderous hordes upon every exposed bit of skin about you.' Waugh recorded that when a local man had been convicted of a serious crime, the laird instructed that he should be 'stripped naked and tied to a stake and left exposed in the sun in that spot till he was stung to death by the gnats and flies'.

Of the trilogy of insect pests, I most feared the sheep-ticks. After a day on the hills, I would toast myself before the fire and become aware of specks of black in the area of my legs, between stockings and 'breeks'. A friend staying at Kinloch Castle unwittingly left a window open and the bedroom light switched on. He returned to his room several hours later to find a host of midges in residence. Campbell Steven, writing in 1955, mentioned the clegs that 'descended on us in their hundred, suicidal in their thirst for human blood. . . . Never in our lives had we experienced mass attacks like these.' The workmen complained that 'if it isn't the midges, it's the clegs, and if it isn't the clegs, it's the rain.'

There is, of course, a brighter side to life on Rhum. When the rain stops and the coolins lose their bonnets of cloud, when the burn's roar becomes a murmur, and sunlight warms the sodden ground, then Rhum is enchanting. Almost all the residents live at Kinloch, beside Loch Scresort, where stand the castle, a school, a hall used for dancing and film shows, and the homes of those who work for the Nature Conservancy Council. Students of deer behaviour occupy an old cottage at Kilmory, where water that has seeped down a marshy glen meets the sea in an area of dunes and links. Red deer frequent the shores and dine on seaweed. It was at Kilmory that I saw a stag with antlers tangled with plastic fishing-net.

Along the wild Atlantic coast are fearsome cliffs, some greatly eroded, culminating with the near-vertical Bloodstone Hill. The cliffs peter out at Harris, an old crofting area now deserted except by red deer, goats and bird migrants like golden plover. Then it's more cliffs, more goats, into the unknown quarter of Rhum, where the golden eagle slices the mist and some of the best seabird colonies are found. South-east, the stern glen of Dibidil holds one of the liveliest of the short rivers. I arrived here soaked, waded recklessly through the river and made for a modest stone building which would offer shelter as I ate my sodden sand-wiches. A family was already in possession – and had just heated up some soup, which they shared with me!

Rhum has variety – lots of deer, a famous herd of ponies and the mountain-top colonies of Manx shearwaters. In recent years, it has acquired sea eagles, as I shall relate. I have climbed Fionchra in mist and rain, settling down to eat my meal at 1,500 feet and marvelling at the speed with which the gulls converged to share the feast. I have ascended Bloodstone Hill, which is not quite as high, and eaten tomato sandwiches in a 'wee shower' – a wretched experience – before standing at the rim of the Sgor Mhor cliffs, which descend a sheer 1,000 feet into the sea. There is bloodstone, a semi-precious stone, on the beach.

The coolins of Rhum, with their vivid Norse names, occupy almost half of the island. There is Askival, the highest point at 2,659 feet, and Hallival, at 2,365 feet, linked by a sharp ridge. No real evidence of Norse habitation has been found. Perhaps the coolins were useful markers as the longships sailed between the islands. Or is the name Trollaval, for one of the peaks, sufficient proof of Norse settlement? It was surely from 'troll', the creature that lived in caves by day and wandered forth at night. Did the screaming of the Manx shearwaters persuade the islanders that Trollaval was occupied by little demons?

In high summer, shoals of mackerel move off-shore, and the gannets arrive to share the feast; a watcher on Rhum sees their gleaming whiteness afar off. The feral goats were mentioned by Pennant, an eighteenth-century visitor, though the old stock may have been augmented by introductions of mainland goats when Sir George Bullough was almost a king on this island. Dr Johnson, in his tour of the Hebrides, was told about the Rhum ponies, which were 'very small but of a breed eminent in beauty'. Those ponies are used for transporting the bodies of deer from the hills to the larder. The Highland cattle are from stock brought across from Mallaig in a landing-craft. The red deer were introduced after the failure of the native stock, at the time when sheep were brought in. The *Old Statistical Account* (1796) associated the demise with the felling of woodland in which the beasts had sheltered. 'While the wood throve, the deer also throve; now that the wood is totally destroyed, the deer are extirpated.'

I saw my sea eagles. They were tethered in an area where few people go, and they could look eastwards, across a tract of wild country towards the Rhum coolins. Being immature, they had not acquired the white tail feathers from which the species was once called 'white-tailed sea eagle'. Nor had their eyes assumed the golden hue from which an old Gaelic name was derived: *iolair shuil na-greine*, 'the eagle with the sunlit eyes'. These birds, brought as nestlings from Scandinavia, would soon be given the freedom of the Hebridean skies. A soaring sea eagle looks so huge it has been described as a 'flying barn door'; the wedge-shaped tail seems to be attached directly to the trailing edges of the wings, as though it was an after-thought.

Hopefully, Britain will be re-populated by sea eagles from the base on Rhum. Under an imaginative scheme of the Nature Conservancy Council, generations of young eagles have been transported from eyries in Norway to the quiet sanctuary, where they grow to independence with regular food supplies and minimal disturbance by man. Already about forty birds have been released, and some are now at the age to nest. It will be a return welcomed by all but sheep-farmers. Well over a thousand years ago, a Northumbrian poet – writing possibly about the Bass Rock – mentioned the sea eagle under its old name, erne, noting that 'full oft the erne wailed round, spray feathered.' Erne, and its many variations, passed into the language of topography. It may be that Unst, the most northerly of the Shetland Isles, was named after the bird.

There was a time when the sea eagle nested in England. What is called Heron Crag, near Haweswater, in the Lake District, must surely have been 'the erne's crag'. Most of the eagle pairs nested by the sea, where they could prey on fish and seabirds. So bountiful was the sea that the eagles became insular; there was no need for them to migrate elsewhere in winter. This trait led to their extinction in Britain. A sea eagle's eyrie was well known, for the bird could hardly skulk. As it became a rare sight, it attracted the attention of egg-collectors and sportsmen seeking trophies. The last pair of sea eagles nested on Skye in 1916. (Nine years before, a gamekeeper on Rhum slew the remaining sea eagles on this wild island.) Once the eagle was lost, there were no convenient replacements, for the Scandinavian birds were just as parochial as the Scottish birds had been.

The sea eagle was yet another species with a hooked bill that was classified as vermin. Harvie-Brown heard from an old man who had been a shepherd on Rhum between 1824 and 1831 that he destroyed a pair of sea eagles, also their three eaglets – an unusually large number. He shot one eagle; it flew towards Skye, then plummeted into the sea. When he shot a female near the nest, the male found another mate. The shepherd promptly slew the second female, and not unnaturally the male deserted. John Woolley, writing in the 1850s, described two islets in a Sutherland loch: 'In each were two or three little trees, and in each was a huge nest of the Sea-Eagle, fixed so near the ground that a child could see into it – one nest some years old, the other repaired that season.'

John Colquhoun, who gloried in his shooting experiences, was on Skye in the 1860s. Sea eagles were 'neither so rare nor so savage as the golden, but, although more vulture-like in their spirits and tastes, are still destructive and ferocious birds. Their liking for fish and water-fowl makes them choose a range in the neighbourhood of the sea or of a freshwater loch. They will not scruple to attack a full-grown goose, although I have never been able to prove their power to lift one. The time for the sea-eagle's fishing is when the warm weather brings its prey to the surface. I have known a shepherd lad secure a good breakfast every day while the eaglets were rearing, simply by watching the feeding hour and robbing the eyrie.' It was Colquhoun, in 1879, who shot one of a pair of eagles nesting near Cape Wrath. The other bird remained faithful to the site for a few more years, and then was seen no more.

Sea eagles fed themselves by flying down seabirds, especially cormorants; they took fish, rabbits, carrion – and any weakly lambs they could find. A pair on Unst in 1868 collected poultry at the cottage doors of Balta Sound when the men were 'awa' at the fishing', 'treating the women and children with the utmost contempt'. Charles Dixon, in 1888, was surprised that the big bird held its own 'in spite of the price set upon its head, and notwith-standing the incessant persecution to which it is subjected by shepherds and gamekeepers'. He had seen the heads and feet of sea eagles nailed in dozens to kennel doors, 'in company with one or two of those of the Golden Eagle, and numbers of Ravens, Buzzards and Peregrines . . .'.

Richard and Cherry Kearton were elated, while standing on a remote cliff, as the local eagle 'gave us a splendid sight by flying leisurely away out to sea and back again over our heads, with the morning sunlight full on it, and a small crowd of unheeded gulls in pursuit'. Cherry, the athletic type, shinned down a rope but found the eyrie empty, 'except for a number of sea eagle's feathers'. It was a surprise to notice that the eyrie was small – just a few sticks and a liberal quantity of moss and dead grass and wool.

In more enlightened times, men dreamed of re-introducing the sea eagle. The Royal Society for the Protection of Birds, in 1968, acquired four eaglets from Norway and set them free on Fair Isle, midway between Orkney and Shetland. A worthy idea founded partly through a shortage of eagles, one of which died after its plumage was clogged by oil spat by an excited fulmar. When the Nature Conservancy Council decided to continue the experiment, using Rhum as a base, the RAF flew the selected eaglets from Norway to Kinloss, from which air station they were transported to Mallaig, thence by ferry to Rhum. In remarkably short time, the eaglets exchanged a ledge on a mountain for an enclosure on a Hebridean hillside.

Of the first batch, a single male died. Females were released in the autumn. John Love, a graduate of Aberdeen University, was given the task of tending the eaglets; he had to work out his own routine, feeding them on dead gulls and crows, setting off in his small boat to catch mackerel and being prepared – when birds had been released – to put out deer and goat carrion until they were judged to be independent.

The hunting eagle, flying low, is an impressive sight. In pursuit of seabirds, it has something of the sparrow-hawk's technique – the low sweep, the surprise appearance, in this case forcing a bird onto the water, then exhausting it by making it dive repeatedly. There is a fanciful Shetland tale of an eagle that caught a halibut, a fish it would not normally be able to lift. The bird sank its talons in the fish, then hung on until its prey was exhausted, at which stage the eagle raised one of its wings (why not both?), which acted as a sail. Both bird and fish were blown to the shore, where the eagle released itself by eating the flesh around its embedded talons! A sea eagle that picked up a child, from the edge of a field on Fetlar, carried that child away. Men working in the same field dashed to the eyrie in time to recover the baby alive!

The number of sea eagles seen in Britain has increased dramatically. In the summer of 1981, from 24 to 26 birds were living free in western Scotland. Sea eagles pair for life; the female incubates two eggs, and at the age of five or six a bird is in breeding condition. The species returns to northern Britain with the backing of the law. Rhum at least has no stock of sheep–and thus no militant shepherds.

Kinloch Castle snuggles in a tract of woodland that distinguishes the big, bare island of Rhum. A visitor walks along the shore, then up the drive, and is confronted by a building that is baronial in scale. I have seen many such places during my walks in remoter parts of the Highlands – so-called shooting-lodges of impressive proportions. When I first entered Kinloch Castle, I half expected to see bare rooms, with rotting wood and crumbling plasterwork. This had been my experience elsewhere. Instead, there was an Edwardian extravaganza, a fully furnished home, immaculately maintained. It was the whim of a wealthy textile magnate in days when income tax was low and anyone with means could draw on the services of a reservoir of cheap labour.

The Bulloughs of Accrington revolutionised the Lancashire cotton industry by their hard work and inventiveness; they became millionaires in the process. John Bullough was friendly with Edwin Waugh, the Lancashire poet, and Waugh told him of a visit paid to the island of Rhum. Bullough was sufficiently interested to rent a shooting-box. That was in 1885, and in the following year he bought the island! (Another prospective pur-chaser was discouraged by a friend, who reported about Rhum: 'Difficult of access, climate abominable, and everything uncom-fortable. Ugh! Ugh! I wouldn't live on the place tho' you gave me it for nothing. . . .')

John Bullough, temporarily free from the stresses of running his textile enterprise, and fidgety – as are most northerners – went seeking the red deer. Lord Salisbury had re-introduced deer to Rhum, and about 600 were present when the Bulloughs took possession. The island was said to have a stock of grouse but, the small number disappointing the new laird, he promptly imported 200 brace! Old John died in 1891, to be succeeded by his eldest son, George, who had just attained his majority. Thrift, a charac-teristic of self-made Lancashiremen, had helped to amass the family fortune. George, who had a privileged upbringing and was educated at Harrow, formed a taste for collecting art trea-sures. He set about spending the family's 'brass'. He toured the world in his yacht *Rhouma* (a splendid boat that was fitted out as a hospital ship during the Boer War, taking up station off Cape Town, where it was used to accommodate injured officers. Large-ly because of his generosity and patriotism, George was knighted in 1901).

Though he was unlikely to spend much time on Rhum, he had the old Kinloch House demolished. He would build something more imposing on the land between two local burns. Money was the least of the problems – even a quarter of a million pounds, which was the sum involved in his plans for Rhum. With no suitable stone on the island, he arranged for red sandstone to be shipped from Arran, 160 miles away. With no soil suitable for a garden, he had top-soil transported from Ayrshire. What Sir George decreed, and a firm of London architects planned, a small army of men put into effect. The workers – masons, joiners, craftsmen of various kinds – were obliged to wear the kilt!

'Castle' is a rather grand title for the building that appears like a mirage among the woodlands of Kinloch (Sir George planted 80,000 trees, of 120 species!). The place is undoubtedly impressive, with the obligatory tower, castellations, even a covered colonnade, a concession to the heavy rainfall. The appearance of the interior makes the most lasting impression. John Betjeman wrote: 'The fittings and furnishings of Kinloch Castle are their own brochure and can show the whole world how a small rich part of it lived in an age which has gone for ever.'

In the Great Hall, light filters through stained glass and the fronds of potted ferns to illuminate a vast space that is decked by varied and rich furnishings. The balcony is adorned with stag heads in traditional style. The walls are hung with portraits of family interest, many of them specially painted to be displayed at Kinloch. Ornaments collected during eastern travels stand about the room, and among the expensive rugs covering the floor are some animal skins.

Here a wealthy man, his family and friends could relax in comfort after a day spent on the wet, cleg-ridden hills. Entertainment was homespun but benefited by the presence of some costly equipment, including a Steinway concert-grand – as good as that to be found in the Usher Hall in Edinburgh – and a mechanical organ of German origin, driven by an electric motor and housed beneath the grand staircase. Only one other organ of this type could be found in Britain, and that was owned by Queen Victoria! The castle has a ballroom with a cut-glass chandelier and minstrels' gallery; bedrooms with four-poster beds; and bathrooms containing what must have been a wonder of the age – a bath-cum-shower, encased in the best mahogany. A panel of taps, connected to what seems to be a mile of lead piping, is the console from which this marvel is controlled. A bather can receive water from several directions and of any desired temperature. One tap is marked 'waves', a boon to those who enjoying sailing toy boats while bathing. That device makes the bathwater as choppy as the sea around Rhum.

Kinloch Castle was in its heyday as a millionaire's home for little more than a decade. The Bulloughs, arriving for the shooting season in their own yacht, brought a house staff to augment the local employees. It was said that the outdoor staff alone peaked at forty, including fourteen full-time gardeners. Outdoors, in good weather, Sir George strolled around the woods and gardens. He visited heated greenhouses where grapes, peaches and figs were grown. He looked at the heated freshwater ponds, in which turtles reclined. For a time, the laird kept a small stock of alligators. The family might stay on Rhum for less than two months.

Sir George died in 1939 and was laid to rest in what must be Scotland's most astonishing mausoleum. Take the (now rough) road from Kinloch across the island to the wild Atlantic coast at Harris, where trees planted some distance from the open sea have been bleached by salt water during fierce storms. Stroll across the grassland of the old crofting community, and suddenly the last resting-place of the Bulloughs is revealed: a Grecian temple, no less, with open sides, its massive roof supported by eighteen cylindrical pillars.

Red deer graze around the structure, sharing the grass with the Highland cattle. And, who knows – as you stand there – you might observe a sea eagle, the 'flying barn door', resting on the wind . . .

# 6

# Isle of Skye:
# A Haunt of Ravens

At 5.30 a.m. there was a throbbing sound, like defective plumb-
ing. I stirred in my bed at the Kyle of Lochalsh. A gull called – not
the usual triumphal sound that awakes even the limpets, but
something of a wail, as though the bird, like me, had been
prematurely roused from sleep. The throbbing could be felt as
well as heard some twenty minutes later; now it reverberated
through my lodgings. The thud of a falling ramp was followed by
the hiss of air-brakes being released and by the over-revving of a
lorry's engines. The ferry service to the Isle of Skye was in
operation.

> Speed, bonny boat, like a bird on the wing,
> 'Onward,' the sailors cry.
> Carry the lad that's born to be King
> Over the sea to Skye.

The bonnie lad of the famous lilt was certainly not waiting for
the ferry to Kyleakin – his sea was the Minch – yet Skye exudes
romance. This was the Norseman's Isle of Cloud, the Gaelic
poet's Isle of Mist, the topographical writer's Winged Isle:
take your pick! Today a utilitarian ferry sweeps across a narrow
stretch of water where once the King of Norway anchored his
galleys. A returning bird-watcher had ticked off the avian
celebrities of Skye: golden eagle, hen-harrier, siskin, ptarmigan, greenshank, raven, hooded crow. It was the raven I was to
remember best.

My excursion began with ravens, which nested on a cliff near
the ancient brochs of Glenelg. On impulse, I left the main road to
the Kyle and crossed Mam Rattigan to the *Ring of Bright Water*
country. While examining the first broch – and the delicate
greenery on the trees round about – I was scolded by a raven. It

58

glided close to the crags, alighted on the rim of the cliff and peevishly tugged up grass and turf, tossing them to the wind.

William Wordsworth, who was no stranger to Scotland, had boyhood exploits in the company of ravens. He knew the elation of peering into a nest while clutching at a tuft of vegetation growing on the rim of the cliff, which was a risky business. Wordsworth described a raven seen near Ullswater in 1805: 'It was not hovering like the kite, for that is not the habit of the bird; but passing onward with a straight-forward perseverance, and timing the motion of its wings to its own croaking. The waves were agitated; and the iron tone of the raven's voice, which strikes upon the ear at all times as the more dolorous from its regularity, was in fine keeping with the wild scene before our eyes.'

The flight of the raven is much more varied that Wordsworth's fine prose suggests; the bird moves directly, with regular wing-beats. During courtship, play or in the presence of strangers, it may soar, dive and sweep in great circles. A raven can surprise the watcher by flipping belly-up, to glide upside down. Ravens launch themselves from a cliff face, locate a thermal and are carried aloft like burnt fragments from a November bonfire.

The raven's appearance matches the cragginess of its haunts. This bird is large, coal-black, with a shaggy throat. The bill, also black, has affinities with a pickaxe. I have watched a raven shatter the rib-case of a dead sheep to reach gobbets of flesh. The birds at Glenelg presumably had young in the nest. Ravens are devoted parents; they vigorously defend their nesting area against most other living creatures, as I was to see on Skye.

I once penetrated a raven's defence system. It was on a day of mist, with showers of hail. The male was grounded, visibility had been reduced to a few yards, and I was undetected in my progress along a sheep-trod, up a scree slope and through a belt of snow to the edge of the cliff the ravens had selected for their bulky, twiggy nest (they tend to change the site from year to year). The female straddled the nest, with wings half-opened, protecting the young birds from hail that was being flung at the family group by a wind full of spite.

A raven's call broke the silence of Glen Eichaig when I walked to the Falls of Glomach, using an estate road and a track that gained and then lost height with a wearying regularity. I fought my way to the heights only to descend steeply to burn-level again. In due course, the path settled down, being little more than a ledge on the side of the hill. I had seen the top of the famous fall from a distance, and only the top was visible when I was quite close to it, so I slithered downhill again and found a vantage-point, near where a toppled tree lay jammed on its side, continuing to throw out lusty growth. The water raced from an upper glen, giving an extra bloom to the grey rocks. A single burn became two large cascades, which tumbled – down, down, down – to a pool where water hissed. The air was chill and vapour rose like steam from a witch's cauldron. The only bird call I remember was the *pruk* of a raven.

In the main glen, the heather's dark shades contrasted with the lemon, orange and light browns of wizened grasses and reeds. The hill looked dead, but life abounded. Red deer, which had visited the riverside flats during the night, were now retreating to the ridges, to chew the cud in obscurity and to escape any insect pests. Blocky stags had cast their antlers. Two fine stags, which a short time before would have met each other, head to head, with interlocked antlers, demonstrating their strength in a glorified boxing match, sorting out some minor problem of superiority, had lost their antlers and contented themselves with rearing on their hind legs to 'box' with the forelegs.

I lunched beside a bright blue lochan. A nestling crow called from a coniferous plantation. A pair of golden eagles, in gliding flight, passed low over a ridge near a mountain pine – the type of strong, isolated tree on which eagles like to nest. Three visitors, stripped to the waist, tottered towards me after visiting the Falls of Glomach; they flung themselves on the ground, providing a banquet for the local sheep-ticks.

Now it was early morning, at the Kyle of Lochalsh. I stood near a patch of flowering gorse and watched the comings and goings of the Kyleakin ferry. An elderly couple from London, part of a coach party and unsure of their position in Britain, believed they were standing near an inlet of the North Sea. A herring-gull called. The old lady swung her head. 'Cor – what's that? A cat?' The gull appeared to laugh. The ferry approached, trying to stir some life into the flat and limpid sea.

The 'far cuillins' were now exerting their appeal. It was the railway that opened up Skye in Victorian times, and those hardy tourists found here a natural playground in which to walk and climb, make lists of birds and flowers and apply paint to canvas, hoping to capture the fleeting moments when clouds parted to allow shafts of light to reach the earth. George Rowntree Harvey wrote: 'Do not be too much taken aback if, when you arrive, one way or the other, there is no Skye to be seen, only seemingly impenetrable grey mist, miles and miles and miles of it, up, down and across. I have a theory that the sun is always shining somewhere in Skye and, certainly, it is as much an island of rainbows as it is of mist. And when a day does come of clear sunshine in Skye, make the fullest use of it.'

James Boswell, in 1773, grimly observed that 'half the year it is deluged with rain. From the autumn to the vernal equinox, a dry day is hardly known.' A lace-pattern designer of Glasgow, named Alexander Smith, spent the summer here in 1862. He must have worn out his umbrella. In four weeks there were four days of 'partial rain'; on the other twenty-seven days, the rain was incessant! Luckily, I arrived on Skye when all was clear and bright. When it does rain, it lays the 'shimmering screen' of midges. As another storm advances, the native remarked: 'Och, but this is the West.'

Skye is a big island: 48 miles long, 24 miles wide. The rising sea that severed it from the mainland runs up numerous sea lochs. Someone with time and patience calculated the length of its shoreline at something over 1,000 miles. There are the Cuillin Hills, of course, asserting – if you were not already aware – that Skye is largely volcanic, a former playground of fire and water. The lavas went cold some 50 million years ago. In the north, where the high ground has the delightful general name of Trotternish, volcanic rock was left with an unstable base of soft clays when the Pleistocene ice had melted; the result is a bizarre countryside, at the Quiraing and Storr, of needle-like rocks and cliffs separated by ravines.

Skye, an island of gentle folk, has a capital in Portree, a fairy-tale castle in Dunvegan, and a scattering of crofting settlements. The peat-diggers of Skye had rolled up their sleeves. They smiled as they lifted turves that were the colour of chocolate cake into neat rows for drying by wind and sunshine. A joiner who was reconstructing a sheep-fank to the north of Portree was actually sweating. Yet another peat-digger, who wore blue overalls, not the kilt, had turned up pieces of birch-bark, remnants of an ancient forest. The modern coniferous plantations are poor compensation for the loss of the old woodlands, with their mix of species and diverse wildlife. The new projects would have been denounced by Wordsworth as 'vegetable manufactory'!

A short-eared owl eyed me from its perch on a fencing post, and later I saw a male hen-harrier – a necessary contradiction if the sex is to be given – in lazy flight over a dark-green stubble of young trees. Skye today is not exceptionally rich in birds, especially seabirds. The sea eagles were 'extirpated'; once there were ten eyries between Loch Brittle and Cop-na-How Head. Some of the old seaside sites are being used by golden eagles.

North of Portree, the skyline was crowned by The Storr and its attendant isolated pinnacle, The Old Man, slightly tilted, as though a rocket had slipped on its launching-pad. The Storr, brushed by clouds at 2,300 feet, is the 'attic' of the Trotternish, those 19 miles of 'tops', from Beinn A' Chearcaill to Shurr Mor. The walker joyfully tramps on airy ridges; the botanist loses his scientific coolness when he locates the Icelandic purslane, with its bright red stem. He may have already found holly fern, saw-wort and northern rock cress.

Storr means 'decayed tooth', which is apt. These teeth are immense. Columns of basalt stand on smooth turf, the sheep being the official green-keepers. We humanise our landscape, giving cosy names to its features. After paying homage to the Old Man – which overhangs its base and does not encourage one to loiter – I went to the coast, and to Kilt Rock, which I found to resemble a truant section of Fingal's Cave on Staffa.

A Sabbatical calm lay over the crofting community of Staffin. No one stirred at the white-washed homes. Tiny fields, the moor and the roads had been given over to the Blackfaced ewes and their new lambs. The few cattle I saw were of the vulgar (black) type, such as those which were driven on the hoof to Kyleakin, swum across to the mainland and taken to the trysts of the lowlands, here to be purchased by the English graziers, for eventual sale at the English markets. I once chatted with an old lady on the Pennines who remembered when her father travelled to the cattle sales in Scotland and arranged for the stock to be driven southwards by Scotsmen. He met them at Alston, paid them for their trouble and left an Englishman and his dog to see the cattle through their final stretch of country, to Wensley-dale.

I turned towards the dark pinnacles of the Quiraing. Parking my car just off the road, close to an old peat-working – and a startled cock wheatear – I trudged uphill to enter the Grand Canyons of Skye: narrow gullies between rock faces that were hundreds of feet high. The Cuithraing, or Pillared Stronghold, has become the Quiraing (to some, Quirang). Some layers of basalt hold evidence of life in remote times: impressions of fossil leaves, interspersed with sediments.

I passed The Needle, which has a height of 120 feet. I found one of the less demanding gullies and climbed close to dark rocks on which were cushions of purple saxifrage in flower. Now I was at The Table, an immense rock overspread with a 'cloth' of fine, close turf, hemmed in by dark crags and pinnacles: an eerie spot which must surely be a habitation of trolls. It was in every sense of the word fantastic.

Finding a sunny patch of ground, close to the lofty cliffs, I settled down to eat. It was then that a raven's call – *rok, rok* – broke the stillness. Soon afterwards I heard the honk of a hooded crow, like the sound made by one of the old bulbous motor horns. A boundary dispute was in progress. The agitated raven soared and called, swooped and called again; it flew beside the cliff with its wing-tip almost brushing the rock. The call, deep in register, with a dry quality, was not loud and yet had tremendous carrying power. The raven broke the skyline and in silhouette offered me a good view of extended primaries, like the fingers of a hand, and a wedge-shaped tail. The raven flipped on its back, resumed the normal position, dived with something of the verve of a falcon and alighted – still vexed – on the rim of the cliff. It was the turn of the 'whoodie' to become demonstrative. A battle of voices, and fine display of flying skills, continued throughout my stay at the Quiraing.

Some of the local ravens nest on seaside cliffs, as they do at Noss, in Shetland. 'Nevver meddle wi' da ravens,' said the old men of Shetland, 'for they are God's birds, His messengers long ago to the holy Elijah.' The Norsefolk revered the raven, and the Lord of the Isles featured it on his crest: 'a raven proper, perched on a rock'. Ravens croaked when rain was imminent, it was said. Long years ago, a crofter approached the governor of the castle at

Eilean Donnan and said that ravens were calling, and so a great storm was in prospect. Could he have the help of some soldiers in securing the harvest? The governor obliged. As the soldiers moved out, the men of Kintail occupied the castle!

On my last day, I travelled to Elgol for a view of the Cuillin Hills with sea in the foreground – a view without which a Scottish calendar would seem incomplete. I passed small herds of Highland cattle, the colours ranging from honey to black. Deciding on the twelve-mile walk to and from Sligachan, by way of Camusunary, I paused at the top of the first long climb and scanned a cluster of islands: Rhum, Eigg, Canna, Sanday, Oskier, even South Uist. Far below, the tide swirled into Loch Scavaig, dissipating its energy on a shallow beach of white sand: a beach littered with plastic trash that had been washed in and left stranded on this lonely shore. Oystercatchers animated the tide's edge; a flock of northern race golden plover settled on the fine turf.

A section of a telegraph pole, scoured and bleached by a thousand tides, was a seat from which I could take a longer look at three of the Small Isles – Eigg, Muck, Rhum. In the bay swam guillemot, red-throated diver and the ubiquitous herring-gull. I entered the gap between Sgurr na Stri and Strathaird. Hills with jagged tops soared around me. Boulders littered the scene. Mist and rain had nourished the vegetation, and there was a fine assembly of rowans. Slow-shifting curtains of vapour seemed incapable of breaking free from the ring of cuillins; they swirled in the eddies, depositing fine snow on the hills. Lawrence Pilkington, a Victorian poet, wrote of 'cliffs frowning on the seas', of 'dark clouds and sudden showers' and of 'mist charged with rainbow light'.

A raven flew through the mist. . . .

# 7

# North-West:
# The Summer Isles and Handa

Red islands? They are not bright red, these fragments of Torridonian sandstone that are stranded off the north-west coast. The
colour appears dull when compared to the red of a tern's bill or a
tystie's legs. The story of the sandstone began some 800 million
years ago with the laying-down of material on an ancient range of
gneissose rocks. Thousands of feet accumulated, to be lifted up,
then savagely eroded. The visual remains are at their best in the
Torridon area.

I had met the sandstone already. A mass of it obtrudes to the
north of Loch Scresort, on Rhum, the beds tilting a little, giving
the impression that they are about the slip under the sea. Now I
was to visit islands and stacks composed entirely of this warm-
looking stone: first an archipelago of little islands spread over
thirty square miles of sea at the entrance to Loch Broom, and then
a blocky island, to the north: a red island lying off a foreland of
grey rock, the Lewisian gneiss. The archipelago is known as the
Summer Isles; the single island is named Handa.

The journey to Ullapool was protracted. I stopped by the
Blackwater to watch four siskins, all male, working their way
through a group of alders. Black heads indicated their sex;
yellow-green bodies were clearly delineated by the dark tones of
the trees. I stopped by Loch Droma to study a black-throated
diver. And I stopped for a view of the Corrieshalloch Gorge,
which was cut by melt-water from an ice cap and is now in the
care of the National Trust for Scotland. Joe Brown, abseiling from
a bridge, went fishing in pools lying between grey and rounded
rocks in a part of the gorge where few people have been.
Fortunately for us all, he was accompanied by a television film
crew.

It was midday when I reached Ulli's Steading, now called
Ullapool. Rows of white-painted houses occupy a beach lying

fifty feet above sea-level. Fishing-boats and their attendant gulls enlivened the day. It is from Ullapool that a large car-ferry sails for Stornaway. Pleasure craft make herring-bone patterns on Loch Broom as they head for the Summer Isles. Ullapool is not a city, but there is no larger settlement further north. It has become a Highland 'honeypot', a point of concentration for tourists.

Ullapool's neat appearance is a tribute to eighteenth-century planning. The place sprang into existence during the great herring boom, and fishermen and fish-curers had their homes here. The British Fisheries Society established this wee town in the Heilands to encourage immigrants. The new Ullapool cost the Society £7,778, and in 1794 there stood here 'a village of 72 houses, 35 slated, the rest thatched with turf, fernroots and heather'. Scotsmen had been slow off the mark in exploiting the herring fishery, and not until 1760 did they seriously challenge the Flemish, Dutch and German vessels which for at least three centuries had operated off the east coast. At the time Ullapool was constructed, the main competition came from the Dutch.

The west-coast fishing stations dated mainly from the mid-eighteenth century, where fish entered the lochs in vast numbers. Less than forty years after the 'planned village' of Ullapool appeared, the effects of over-fishing were everywhere evident. The catches diminished; the curing industry faded. Yet in its heyday, scores of ships might be seen in the bay, and salted herring was being exported to Russia, Germany and lands around the Mediterranean.

From a hill above Ardmair Bay, a little to the north of Ullapool, I watched the weather deteriorate. For a time, Ben More Coigach was in clear view and, beyond it, the big bens. The birds were quietly industrious: hooded crows on the beach, eiders at the sea's edge, a red-throated diver half-submerged as it swam far out. A cool breeze swept the hilltop; then a few grey clouds smudged the blue sky to the south-west. Thunderclaps were to be heard. The clouds thickened; the hills darkened; the sea lost its lustre. Rain fell like water from a celestial hosepipe. There is nothing like a spell of heavy rain to calm a choppy sea. Even so, the skipper of *The Islander* was astonished that a score of people booked for the journey to Carn nan Sgeir, one of the smallest of the Summer Isles.

What's in a name? Pennant, writing in 1772, thought the

appearance of the Summer Isles was dreary and that they were misnamed. Fraser Darling mentioned that these islands, like many others, were grazed by domestic stock in summer, a reasonable explanation of the name the Summer Isles until another authority claims that the isles of the *sunn maer* were the isles of the 'south border'.

Darling wrote of his experiences on the Summer Isles in a charming book called *Island Farm*. That farm stood on Tanera, the largest of the group. He referred to the cattle husbandry of the Highlands, then more or less dead, for sheep had taken the place of cattle, 'so that now the Summer Isles might be more correctly named the Winter Isles. The weaned lambs of the mainland crofters' flocks are put to the islands in October and brought back in February or early March.' He inquired into the history of the Little Irish Park and discovered a relationship with the old herring industry. When part of the catch cured in Tanera was exported to Ireland, boats came back in ballast with Irish soil, which was dumped and spread in this little field.

Less well known is F. Fraser Darling's little book called *Wild Country*, published in 1938 (by Cambridge University Press) and containing a section on Eilean A' Chleirich, outlying island of the Summer Isles group, where something of the author's contentment with island life is revealed.

It is true that it is bare and we can see no woods; but leave the great spaces of land and sea and consider this little island (Eilean A' Chleirich) with its lochans and its green places. Consider this spot. I am lying in sunlight by lapping water, where bright green blades of flags come through the sodden ground at the water's edge. Here is a tiny rowan tree in leaf, making a continual change of pattern against the sky as the breeze crosses its leaves. Bracken is uncurling all round me, and I can see the blue carpet and smell the sweet nostalgic scent of the blue-bells – surely a great forest of beauty, A brilliantly coloured fly hovers before the bells of a flower and settles on the stalk. I am struck by its iridescence in the sunlight.

Where is the bareness and poverty? Through the warp of green and blue, of stalk and flower, I see the different blue of the rippled lochan; beyond, the more intense blue of the sea; and, farther still, the mainland with its tiny white houses in a patchwork of crofts, backed by the slopes of the mountains and their stony summits. I am looking through the immediate and minute to the far distant and immense, and my eyes come back again to the luxuriance of growth in this small patch. The wheatears chatter among the stones and flirp their tails, the insects hum, the water laps continuously. In this scent-laden sunshine I might fall asleep.

Priest Island, 300 acres, with caves and cliffs rising to 100 feet, plus several small lochs, is a reserve of the RSPB. The island has been uninhabited by man for over a century. Bird life is profuse, with an estimated 10,000 pairs of storm-petrels, nesting in holes in scree and peat bank. This may be the largest colony of storm-petrels in Britain.

*The Islander* cruised near the cliffs of the southern shore. Raindrops bounced off the oil-rich plumage of the sitting fulmars. As time passed, the sun did not reappear but the rain stopped. My clothes began to steam. The land masses were now in pastel shades, and mist floated among the hills as though trying to find an escape route. The boat was drawn up against a ridge of jagged rock on Carn an Sgeir.

There are really two islands, linked by a storm beach on which terns have been known to nest. The air is clear, as indicated by the splashes of bright lichen. Orange, grey and black lichen form a patchwork on the cliffs, and flowers scent the air. Here is scurvy grass, sea pink, sea campion, chickwood, patches of great woodrush and some lovage. The grass is fine and smooth, being grazed by sheep, rabbits and the Greenland barnacle geese that visit these islands to feed, preen and rest, leaving their substantial droppings, like offerings to the goddess of fertility.

I disturbed an eider duck; the bird scurried away from a nest that held a partly completed clutch of eggs, with a little down as lagging. From secure and well provisioned bases on the northern and western isles of Scotland, the eider began a remarkable spread during the nineteenth century. An estimated 2,000 pairs nest on the Sands of Forvie, in the east, and the west-coast colonies extend as far south as Walney Island, off Cumbria. Herring-gulls were nesting on Carn nan Sgeir, and the birds called peevishly as they circled. Shags were there, occupying ledges near the sea, screeching and moving their heads from side to side if I ventured too close to their nest.

*The Islander* returned to Ullapool on a sea that had a milky appearance. Tysties, nervously strained, dipped their heads in the water. The Summer Isles, grey in mist, were like a battle fleet assembled for inspection.

Wedge-shaped Handa has a pronounced list towards the east, giving the impression that it was scuttled and came to rest scarcely a mile from the mainland. Handa is 1½ miles long, about a mile wide, and rises to a little over 400 feet at Sithean Mor (the Great Hill of the Fairies). The wee folk must have had their gossamer wings shredded by gales on this exposed coastline. Handa, the 'sandy isle', is least impressive when viewed from the mainland, across a narrow sound that is dotted with skerries, on which the tysties nest. Boats making the short, not always smooth, crossing from Tarbet ride the waves onto a beach of white sand. The main footpath crosses an expanse of turf and peat to the brink of cliffs where the Torridonian sandstone is stratified horizontally, providing nesting quarters for some 100,000 seabirds. Until 1864, the sea eagle lived here.

In early June, I followed the rolling Scottish road to where I might embark for Handa. My route was a wilderness way, between hills with bald pates, near a lochan or two of such an intense blue that I wondered if someone had topped them up with dye. I saw the emergent flag iris, a plant that is to this northern landscape what daffodils are to the Lake District. The *Puffin*, a small open boat with an outboard engine, stirred some movement into slack water and caused a tystie to dive, its scarlet legs being visible as it plunged.

The boat swung towards Port an Eilean, a name which sounds impressive but is merely a sandy bay. The engine was cut. Waves provided the impetus for the final approach, and I stepped, half dazzled, onto a sunlit beach composed of pure white sand. White beach, turquoise sea, powder-blue sky: this area needed only a few palm trees to complete the illusion of being in the Caribbean. If the edge of the sea looked muddy, it was not mud but fine sand in suspension – sand stirred by waves that broke on a steep shore. Before another wall of water flopped onto the beach, the particles had sunk, and all was clear and lovely again.

It is a treacherous coastline, even in the lee of Handa. Two boatmen were drowned a few years ago. In 1977, when the summertime warden of the RSPB arrived to take up his duties, over two days elapsed before he could be transported to the island, and in the nine following days, so unsettled was the weather that he did not see another soul. A good friend of mine collapsed and died on the beach at Handa, within a few paces of the boat. For years, thoughts about this remote island and its seabirds had influenced his reading and coloured his dreams. He planned a fortnight's holiday, the culmination of which would be a landing at this remote spot. Postcards from him told of his northerly progress; he crossed the Sound of Handa – and died from the effects of a heart-attack within moments of landing.

The RSPB has run Handa as a nature reserve for twenty years, which is simply a wink in the long story of human occupation. Tombstones, set in the damp ground, remind us of the time when seven families lived here, subsisting on fish and potatoes, a diet they would surely supplement by seabirds and their eggs. The oldest widow on Handa was proclaimed the 'queen'. Men met each morning, as the local Parliament, to plan the day's activity. In 1845, the Handa potato crop failed and, faced with famine, the people vacated their homes in the spring of 1848. A few weeks later, when Charles St John visited Handa, he saw their 'several huts' on which 'the turf walls were already tenanted and completely honeycombed by countless starlings.' From time to time, shepherds patched up the buildings and occupied them for a few weeks.

A path led me gently across the almost empty heart of Handa. In places, the path had been reinforced by boards. Wheatears chacked alarm – some thirty pairs nest on Handa – and a meadow pipit displayed. I saw a great skua, the celebrated 'bonxie', trimming its wings and tail to the light breeze. Bonxies and Arctic skuas returned to breed on Handa at about the time it became a nature reserve. A pair of divers usually nests on the lochan. When, in 1975, the water level rose nearly six inches after a 'wee shower', the warden noticed the plight of the divers and their threatened nest. He moved the diver's egg to a drier platform of grass and moss. In 1964, a plantation was established, and the willow-warbler and redpoll could be added to the Handa list of nesting species.

A whiff of air soured by seabird droppings was my first hint of the approach of the bird cliffs. I stood on the rim and had the dizzying sensation of looking down, down, down, to where the sea was dashing itself against pink slabs and stacks. Fulmars fought to maintain their position against the uprushing wind; the birds hung, with dangling feet, bracing their wings, fanning out their tails. A large seabird colony transmitted its special feeling of excitement. I heard the growling and grunting of innumerable auks and saw a blizzard of white feathers as kittiwakes circled and screamed. A hundred thousand birds, of some 30 species, nest on Handa. Statistics are a poor substitute for experience, but the island holds 30,000 pairs of guillemots, 6,000 pairs of razorbills, 7,000 pairs of kittiwakes, 2,000 pairs of fulmars, up to 500 pairs of puffins and 50 pairs of great black-backed gulls, along with several hundred pairs of herring-gulls. On the rocky shore are oystercatchers, ringed plovers and rock pipits. Skuas nest in the hinterland, where the ground is tinted by patches of deer-grass, purple moor-grass and cotton-grass: a real Highland mix. Cheviot sheep graze between bright masses of sea pinks.

The cliff-nesters form an astonishing assembly of crouching, sitting, incubating, defecating, whirring, wheeling birds. They cling to ledge, crack, cranny and knob of rock immediately above an ever-restless sea. A precarious life was made hazardous for them in the old days, when visitors to Handa voyaged round the island. The mate of the boat fired a musket, causing a mass evacuation of the birds – and a shower of eggs, though no one worried about it then. John Macculloch reported that the effect was 'as if a feather bed had been opened and shaken in the breeze'.

Guillemots steal the show by sheer force of numbers. Hamish MacInnes, writing about a rock-climbing venture to the Great Stack of Handa, was reminded as he looked back at the main island of 'tiers of seats in a great opera house, with the birds in their gleaming dinner jackets'. Guillemots, so tolerant of physical contact, can achieve a high breeding density. The eggs do not vary so much in size as in appearance, and the patterning appears to be unique to each egg, a distinct help to the bird when, arriving back at a ledge, it is confronted by more than one egg. The collectors of eggs in Victorian times filled case upon case with specimens of guillemot eggs that were markedly different from each other.

Handa does not immediately reveal all its attractions. Round the corner lay The Great Stack (or Stac), a remnant of the old shoreline. This 80-feet-high Sandstone column stands on five immense legs. One day, the sea will completely undermine the stack; meanwhile, the tides surge under and around it, to smack their lips against cliffs in a geo (creek). A party of Victorians who decided to visit the top of the Great Stack dragged one end of a 600-feet-long rope around the geo, and thus over the Stack, enabling some of them to shin across the gap. Tom Patey used a similar method in 1967, though his rope was made of nylon, and it sagged 40 feet, so that he had to resort to *jumars*. When he reached the halfway point, he saw a guillemot pecking at the rope. He was then squirted by a fulmar! Hamish MacInnes and friends climbed directly from a boat, having discovered a route up the side of the Stack. He recalled: 'We hardly encountered a nest on the ascent, but on the east face it was like Manhattan, the background cries of the birds being deafening.'

I progressed along the clifftops marvelling at the concentrations of seabirds. Guillemots growled – *arrrrr, arrrrr* – as they stood on ledges, where fetid accumulations of droppings were to be seen. Kittiwakes screamed – *kitti-waak, kitti-waak* – as though to identify themselves in the presence of any novice bird-watchers. In the bright light, the cliffs looked pink, capped with verdant green, backed by the strong blues of sea and sky. I passed a natural shaft, connected to a sea cave, which on the wildest days must become a gigantic blow-hole. A bonxie in recline lumbered into the air and sailed the air currents, showing off its white wing patches. An Arctic skua cruised offshore, then put in a spurt to harass a kittiwake.

As the cliffs became smaller during my walk along the southern rim of Handa, I could move with confidence to within a few yards of recumbent guillemots. I followed the progress of some auks as they swam underwater, using their stiffened wings like the flippers of a penguin. The streamlined head and body offered little resistance to the water; webbed feet controlled the bird's movements. On the initial dive, air bubbles trapped in the plumage gave the birds a silvery sheen.

Back on the mainland, I sat in a garden drinking strong tea and eating crab sandwiches as yet another party of bird-watchers sailed for the red island.

# 8

# Durness:
# Sorties in the Far North

Inland, where the last phase of glaciation might have occurred the day before yesterday, stood the big bens, highpoints of the 'knob and lochan' country, and themselves humbled by glacial ice, by wind, rain and frost. I looked at the eroded stumps of what had been much nobler mountains. Elsewhere, the landscape appeared to have sunk, or at least to be awash. Lochans, bogs and moorland, the bogs tufty with cotton sedge, the moors ribbed by peat workings: this was Sutherland, in the Far North of mainland Britain.

Yet 'Sutherland' is a name derived from a Norse source, meaning 'the South Land' – south in relation to the northern isles, which the Norsemen had overrun. Norse names are the language of topography. There is Tongue, from *tunga*, meaning a tongue of land; and Eriboll, from *eyrr bol*, or Beach Town. Durness is 'the point of the wild beast', and Inchard is 'the meadow loch'. Laxford is derived from *lax*, or salmon, for which it is still famous.

The rocks are of gneiss, being pink and grey, the earliest of them laid down over 2,200 million years ago – give or take a few decades. An early traveller noted that 'the country is everywhere deformed by the rocky mountain, the sterile moor and the dangerous brown morass.' The Rev. James Hall, crossing The Moine in 1807, was reminded of Lapland, and a guidebook writer of 1934 mentioned the road to Durness as proceeding 'through a strange chaos of rocks and lochs'.

At Rhiconich I was at the northern edge of Reay Forest, over which the chiefs of the Clan MacKay hunted. From Rhiconich, a modest hamlet, there were thirteen miles of travel through an acid wilderness to the Promised Land – Durness. Here the landscape suddenly brightened. It was not just the effect of light from the sea, but the occurrence of limestone, a sweet filling in the dark geological sandwich of the north-west. Limestone truly sweetens the landscape, and in the afternoon sunlights I saw the drystone dykes were gleaming. These dykes, or walls, bordered fields of sappy grass. This was farming as I knew it, not the traditional crofting. The grass was hardly tall enough to conceal a sparrow, but marsh marigolds flowered in the ditches, mountain avens covered rocky places, and the best land held a constellation of daisies.

A pair of greenshanks resided in a swampy hollow a mere five minutes walk from the Far North Hotel at Balnakeil; common gulls settled on the hotel lawn in the confident expectation of being fed. The hotel is part of a complex of buildings that was part of a radar station of the 1939–45 war, and most of the premises are now being used by craftsmen. Down the road were structures of much greater antiquity. I located a tombstone in the churchyard on which a deer had been roughly outlined. The old mansion across the road was used by the bishops of Caithness when they visited Durness to hunt the deer.

Thoughts of red deer must have coloured the dreams of local people in those distant times. Barley cakes, kail and salt meat formed a monotonous local diet. The people drove their stock to the hills for summer grazing, sustaining themselves the while by drinking milk and curds, whey and preparations made from oatmeal. Bishop Pococke, in 1760, noted there was a new-fangled tuber called the potato; less than a century later, the root was being widely grown. Then it became blighted. The 'potato famine' led to the break-up of many old communities and to widespread emigration.

There was time enough after dinner at the Far North Hotel to become acquainted with the local bird life. I triggered off the early warning system of the birds, including a penetrating series of whistles from the greenshank. *Tu-tu-tu*, was the cry, uttered at a pitch that might shatter a wine-glass. The cock bird, which I glimpsed from afar, had particularly dark wings and used a lichen-plated boulder as a perch. One day, both birds, occupying the same large boulder, scolded me in unison with an oft-repeated *tyip*. A red-throated diver cruised on the lochan, common gulls nested on an islet, a corncrake uttered its double-rasp, and 'comic' terns flew by, some of them bearing small fish in their red mandibles. One day a bonxie flew along the Kyle of Durness, startling both birds and bird-watcher.

I walked beside 'meadows' of mountain avens here growing almost at sea-level, and noted water avens, bog bean, mountain everlasting, twayblade, alpine bistort, fairy flag. The coastline was distinguished by the Scottish primrose, with its tiny purple-red flowers. It was at home in a sodden landscape. Golden plover whistled from the largest fields. Three tortoiseshell butterflies pressed themselves against a sunlit stone in a sheltered spot, their wings widespread, absorbing all the available heat, for the air was kept cool by a north-westerly wind.

With a dedicated ornithologist called Mike, I decided that the corncrake would be a bird of special study. In Scotland, the survivors of a once great population of corncrakes are found mainly on the islands, and especially on South Uist, where a nature reserve was created with these birds partly in mind. Mike and I pondered on the decline, which is generally associated with changes in farming techniques. The corncrake as a species has long been subjected to numerical fluctuation along the edges of its range. It became quite common last century. Will it adapt to the new order on the land? Our answer was: probably not. Durness revived my old interest in this surreptitious bird, which migrates to Scotland and then seems disinclined to use its wings. The corncrake makes a loud noise but is not often seen. Charles St John, writing of the bird in 1872, thought its call sounded 'as if it was produced by some brazen instrument'. At dawn, he watched a female with young, 'quaint-looking, long-legged young ones', all walking in the same stooping position. Charles St John shot anything that took his fancy. He related that 'the landrail (another name for the corncrake) is in good order on his first arrival, and being then very fat and delicate in flavour, is very good eating.'

The corncrakes return in May, when yellow iris provides the birds with cover until the spring flush of growth has developed. Near Durness, Mike and I found corncrakes using the cover of nettle patches at the edges of the fields. If we walked within a field, lightly touching the nettles with a stick, the corncrake sometimes showed itself, scurrying to yet more cover, rarely using its chestnut wings. Our best spell of observation was on a day spent visiting Oldshoremore, a crofting community at the coast. The bay offered the prospect of fine open beaches, and there was a promontory composed of the now familiar warm red sandstone. Three men, in a small boat that danced on sparkling water, were paying out a salmon net. Other impressions of Oldshoremore were of buildings roofed with corrugated iron and painted red; a stack of really dry peat; a fishing-net hung out to dry; rough stones built into dykes that now were so low they were reinforced with posts and wire; flower fields and 'rush bobs'. Globe flowers jostled each other near the houses and poured down the hillsides in their yellow-topped thousands.

On that hot afternoon, the rasping call of a corncrake might have come from a giant cricket. (We had begun to associate corncrakes with the darker hours.) This bird's territory absorbed two former fields that were now separated by a broken dyke. The ground offered the bird plenty of cover; it was ragged with nettles, thistles and drifts of globe flowers. A hillside provided us with a vantage-point.

The corncrake called at intervals of from two to five minutes, from 2 p.m. to 3 p.m. In a spell of an hour and a half, it moved a mere thirty yards, crossing the tumbled wall. When walking, the bird resembled a chicken keeping its head down, stopping periodically to maintain a fixed position, then – chickenlike – lunging to collect insects from the flower heads. It stood in a patch of thistles with its head up, neck outstretched, following every sound with a crisp movement of its head. When the bird was calling, that head was inclined at about 45 degrees and the wings were partly open. We got the impression that it had puffed out its plumage.

In limestone country, such as Durness, the wee burns have the perplexing habit of flowing underground. Water, collecting a weak solution of acid from the atmosphere and soil, erodes any lines of weakness. The Allt Smoo, a modest watercourse that flows northwards, goes to ground in the caverns of Smoo Cave, which is named after the Norse *smuga*, meaning a hole. When it has gone out of sight, the burn takes an eighty-feet leap into an immense cave, reappearing in a high-sided creek that leads directly to the sea. Walter Scott noted: 'A water kelpie or an evil spirit of aquatic propensities could not have chosen a fitter abode and, to say the truth, I believe at our first entrance, and when all our feelings were afloat at the novelty of the scene, the unex-pected splashing of a seal would have routed the whole dozen of us.' Fulmars cackled near the cave mouth and on the grey ledges beside the creek.

There was no novelty for me in walking through the great arch, over 50 feet high, into the first vaulted chamber of Smoo Cave, for I live in the district of 1,000 caves and potholes. Smoo Cave, with its rent in the roof, reminded me of Gaping Gill on Ingleborough where I have descended by bosun's chair: 240 feet in perhaps 20 seconds, dangling like a spider on a thread under the dome of St Paul's. Smoo has three chambers, the second and third being difficult of access. In the 1850s, local boatmen charged 15s. a time – with an extra charge for lights – when they conducted visitors into the flooded second chamber. Charles Weld wrily observed: 'The game is not worth the candle.'

I looked across a mile of troubled water to the island of Eilean Hoan, where sheep are grazed in summer and the barnacle geese drop in to graze in winter. Eilean Hoan extends to only a hundred acres. I heard vague talk of storm-petrels nesting there. For many years, talk about the features of this north-western corner of Scotland was vague. The cartographer Sir Robert Gordon, visiting Sutherland in the seventeenth century, surveyed Faraid Head, north of Durness, believing that there was no more land to the west. He was not aware of the existence of Cape Wrath!

Faraid Head has about it a feeling of being the ultimate point. There is a desert zone – an area of shifting sand – leading to a headland where the blocky rocks might have been squared up by quarrymen. While walking in the sandy area, I noticed that sand as fine as that in an hour-glass had spilled over the old military road. This hot Scottish desert was given a touch of life by the wheatears; their chacks and whistles punctuated my walk.

I strode to the tip of the headland, where kittiwakes called and shags sat morosely on their nests, some of which had been freshly adorned with greenstuff brought from the sea. There were off-shore stacks, some of which were tiered and whitened, resembling wedding-cakes. The whitewashing was the work of many auks. I sat where terraced grassland swept down to the sea, a terracing produced by natural causes – a shift of the ground. Aldermanic puffins were exchanging pleasantries in the sunlight. Everyone laughs at the puffin, though it is in every respect a serious-minded bird. We laugh at its dumpy appearance, its vertical stance when on land, its rolling walk. We smile at the 'dress suit' and effect of black upperparts and white underparts, half-expecting it to have a chain gold watch at its waist. The flattened, multi-coloured beak looks preposterous; it glows with red, yellow and blue. Yet life is no laughing matter to the puffin. The bird spends most of its life being tossed about on the North Atlantic, and from the moment it touches down on land it has a nesting routine that is beset with difficulties.

It is a true northerner, nesting on either side of the Atlantic, from Greenland to Novaya Zemlya. In winter, the bird wanders freely. Two young puffins 'ringed' on St Kilda were recovered off Newfoundland during the following winter. The puffin's basic nesting requirement is an elevated area of peaty ground or scree slope that is handy to the sea. The white egg is deposited in a crack, among boulders or in a burrow, and when taking flight this high-winged bird likes an immediate uplift from the wind as it fans the coastline. A puffin looks uneasy in flight, whirring its wings, using its webbed feet for steering or as air-brakes. With the sea close at hand, it has a regular supply of fish food – a multitude of little fish, brought to the nest at the rate of a dozen or more when there is a hungry young bird in the burrow.

When the puffins return, there is a carnival spirit on the coast. A few birds appear on the sea, the vanguard of a host of puffins. Rafts of birds float off shore, as though waiting for some brave bird to set foot on land. Many of the puffins have already paired; they rub beaks; they copulate on the water, the males standing with whirring wings on the backs of the partly submerged females, who after mating indulge in ritualised bathing.

The puffins come timorously to land. A few wary, excitable birds alight on the sheep-cropped turf. The slightest disturbance sends them buzzing off to sea. Gradually the birds build up their old confidence at being ashore. Pairs stand about. There is much nibbling of head and neck. A male gallantly presents the female with a token – a feather or a tuft of grass – as a gentle hint that nesting might begin. In territorial disputes, the offended puffin faces the intruder with its beak held low: a sure sign of defiance, not of submission. The warning is usually sufficient to deter the stranger. Battling between birds of the same species is wasteful.

I have watched puffins renovating their burrows. The tough, horny beak is an excellent implement for digging. The legs of the bird are short and strong, the webs of the feet adorned by formidable claws that can send earth flying from a burrow. The female's single egg is spherical, unlike the pear-shaped egg of the guillemot dropped on a precarious and narrow ledge above the sea. The puffin's egg has nowhere to roll. Brooding takes place for forty days and forty nights. It is then that the appearance of a puffinry can be deceptive during the day. The site seems deserted; there are one or two puffins standing around, as puffins do, but most of the birds are either keeping eggs warm or seeking food far out at sea. Most of the aerial activity is observed in the early morning and evening, when the birds swarm like bees from a hive, their dark mantles blending with the cliffs in shadow, the white underparts gleaming.

The bird hatching from an egg is covered with down, being a tousled copy of the adult's plumage, dark above, light below, on a dumpy body. There is need for a large and regular supply of fish. The puffins organise a shuttle service, flying out to sea, pitching down on the waves in areas where food is plentiful. They 'fly' underwater to collect sand-eels and use the utmost economy of movement by contriving to return to the nest with several fish at a time, assembled between the mandibles of that remarkable beak, all lying crossways, sometimes packed alternately, head to tail.

The incoming puffins, with fish glistening in their horny beaks, must run the gauntlet of hungry gulls, which long since discovered that it is easier to rob a bird of fish than go through the tedious occupation of looking for a meal for themselves. Skuas have been known to attack rafts of puffins on the sea, glorying in the kill, as do foxes in a chicken run, destroying more birds than their appetites demand. The puffin arrives at speed, stalls above its burrow and descends almost vertically with fluttering wings. The red feet are held stiffly downwards, and as soon as they touch the ground the bird scurries into the burrow, scarcely looking around. A predatory bird exploits every weakness, and the great black-backed gull has a noxious habit of standing beside a puffin's burrow and capturing the bird as it emerges, deftly turning it inside out and gulping down the most edible parts.

A growing puffin needs fish of a larger size, and the parents oblige. Eventually it is taking its own weight in food each day. For some forty days the food supply continues to arrive, being eagerly received by the young puffin and also by the many insect pests that must make the hot summer days a trial. The adult birds lose the urge to deliver food, and the youngster is left to its own devices. There are also deep-set instinctive responses. For perhaps a week it remains in the burrow. It is nowhere near fully grown when it departs for the sea. A dark night is chosen for the departure: the sort of night favoured by shearwaters and petrels. The youngster blunders through the darkness, negotiating obstacles, fluttering from the heights, questing for the sea. At first light, rapacious gulls eat any young puffins they can find.

The northerly wind persisted at Durness. That wind came fresh from the Arctic, which was the next landform to the north. It was a day for Loch Eriboll: on such a day Loch 'Orrible. Walter Scott came gratefully ashore here during his voyage around the northern lights. His bird-watching was while peering along the barrel of a gun. He wrote: 'Take the fowling piece and shoot some sea-fowl and a large hawk of uncommon appearance. . . . Fire four shots and kill three times.' He visited a house by Loch Eriboll and enjoyed 'an ample Highland breakfast' with 'excellent new-taken herring, equal to those of Loch Fine, fresh haddocks, fresh eggs and fresh butter, not forgetting the bottle of whisky and bannocks of barley and oat-cakes, with the Lowland luxuries of tea and coffee'.

Loch Eriboll had only just come into view when I had the day's most memorable sighting. A pine-marten appeared when I was least expecting it. There is not much to report – the beastie bounded over a tract of heather and took sanctuary among rocks. And that was that! Yet a mental picture remains of its lithesome manner, its glowing fur and bushy tail. By the pier at Partnancon, an eider duck spun in the shallows, stirring up food for its black downy young. A small crèche had assembled near the shore. A sandpiper gave a rippling trill and alighted with a flurry of wings, its body continuing to flick with an excess of nervous energy. Herons contemplated the Loch's shallows without perceptible movement. They might have been turned, by some process of Highland magic, into pieces of grey wood.

The Sutherland of the picture-books is that area known as The Moine, which sprawls, patchy with cotton grass, lacerated where beds of peat are exposed. Someone was faced with the awesome task of making a road across this wild and soggy tract. Bundles of coppice wood were laid in courses, and turf and gravel were piled on top, drains and ditches being cut to release the bog water. A'Mhoine remains sinister; the lochans are as dark as Stephen's

Watching shags on an island in the Firth of Forth

Tantallon Castle and Bass Rock, at the mouth of the Firth of Forth

Muckle Flugga and Outstack, the most northerly rocks, as seen from the Shetland island of Unst

A great skua, the celebrated 'bonxie', dives at an intruder near its nest on Hermaness, nesting ground of both the great and Arctic skuas

Wheatears may be found nesting close to the sea. On Fairaid Head, near Durness, they enliven a sandy waste. A burrow is often selected for the nest

A walker by a sea loch, or on an island, is likely to see the common sandpiper, which flies low over water with quick beats of its wings interspersed with short glides

*(Above left)* A young guillemot, on an island in the Firth of Forth. Long before the bird is fully grown it will have joined its parents on the sea, paddling towards the Norwegian coast. The journey to the sea is usually made in the late evening

*(Above)* A young herring gull 'freezes' on a sandy beach, where its cryptic coloration may ensure that it is overlooked by predators

*(Left)* A diminutive ringed plover chick among the sea-washed pebbles. Large and well-developed legs enable it to move briskly, if speed is necessary

The Bullers of Buchan, on the breezy east coast of Scotland, where some of our largest kittiwake colonies are established. The sea has eroded an amphitheatre which is 50 feet wide and has a depth of 200 feet. The flow tide surges into the amphitheatre through a natural rock arch

Kittiwake at its nest with two well-grown young. After the nesting season, kittiwakes disperse widely over the North Atlantic. Once persecuted for its feathers, the kittiwake is now much more numerous than it was, and it is slowly extending the southern part of its vast breeding range

A demonstrative fulmar and mate

The gannets of Bass Rock. They nest on 350-feet-high cliffs and have also spread across the top of the island, adjusting their lives to the loom of the lighthouse and the occasional deep roaring of the foghorn. The photograph below left shows the bird's binocular vision, by which it can easily locate shoaling fish

Shags on Bass Rock, during a period of foggy weather

The nest of a pair of shags seems only a stage removed from a compost heap and is constantly augmented. Shags nest as close as they dare to the sea

ink. Greenshanks do their best to infuse some life into this rolling landscape.

Tongue is a pleasant spot, in a fertile area by the sea. The protracted approach along the loch side is no longer used by tourists, a bridge and causeway leading them directly to the place. The causeway links some islets, and there is novelty in parking the car and watching, from a range of a few yards, such birds as Arctic tern, oystercatcher and ringed plover, all nesting in their traditional haunts. My appearance put the birds into flight. Then an arctic tern alighted at the merest scrape in which its eggs had been laid. The bird stretched its wings high before tucking them neatly away, by which time it had settled on the eggs.

The oystercatcher stalked up the beach with frequent stops to look round. Then it slipped over its nest, shuffled its plumage and contemplated whatever oystercatchers have in mind when brooding eggs through the long Highland day. A ringed plover zigzagged on twinkling legs: a diminutive bird, cryptically coloured. I had a moment of anxiety as it approached the nest. Would it be able to cover the eggs, which looked huge in comparison with the bird's modest size? With a special effort, it did! Terns jerked their way about the sky, screaming *kee-yair*, and, backlit by sunshine, appeared in translucent splendour.

Waves struck the cliffs near Melness with a dull boom and sheets of spume. Walls of water, green and white, advanced to their destruction a few yards from where I sat, contemplating first the sea then the flowers: squill, lesser butterfly orchid, butterwort, lousewort, globe flower and, a little way off, the inconspicuous rosettes of the Scottish primrose. Suddenly, it was summer! The clouds parted, the lowlands were emerald, with patches of gold where the gorse was massed. The terns celebrated the return of bright conditions by plunge-diving in a bay that held the long, low forms of divers and a few tysties.

Birchwoods lay in a river valley near Ben Hope, and two merlins – first identified as cuckoos! – were in dashing flight. Greenshank called as though proclaiming the Last Judgement. I found yellow pimpernel, cow-wheat (which is semi-parasitic), and chickweed wintergreen – neither a chickweed nor a wintergreen. It had become a day on which to climb Ben Hope, the most northerly of the 3,000-feet 'tops' in Scotland. The path followed the banks of a burn tumbling over a thousand mini-falls and emanating from a rocky arena. A golden eagle soared. A cock ring-ouzel, our white-bibbed mountain blackbird, departed with a clattering alarm call. Beyond the heather lay a tilting world of coarse grasses and grey, lichened rocks. The air seemed cooler with every footfall. Mist took the edges from the distant views.

A hen ptarmigan staged a distraction display, shuffling along the ground with partly open wings, the plump body brushing the ground. There might have been short stumps for legs. This grey-and-white bird was at home among the cold grey boulders. Some twenty yards away, the cock ptarmigan was nervously fidgeting; when I moved towards it, the bird departed with a cackle and a flurry of white wings. Scattered about the hillside, keeping low and still, were the downy chicks. Already their stubby wings were beginning to feather.

The track to the summit of Ben Hope was notable for the number of 'blind summits', and the path terminated with a cairn set in a rockscape. It might be spring in the glens, but up here the air had a wintry chill. Charles Cordiner, the Episcopal minister at Bank, made the ascent in the eighteenth century, using a pony.

At first the mist only obscured the view, but felt chilly as we advanced. When we began to open the horizon beyond, sudden gusts of wind came down between the cliffs into which the summit of the mountain is divided; and the clouds were tossed about into eddies by the squalls until they fell in showers of mingled sleet and rain. It became intensely cold. The current of air, loaded with these embryo-snows, was extremely penetrating. We quickened our pace to get beyond the highest part of our route, and soon found the difficulty of surmounting Ben Hope was over, and that we got into the milder climate again.

# 9

# Cape Wrath:
# The Turning Point

Scotland's remotest cape is much harder to reach than John o' Groats, which has long been thought of as the ultimate destination on the mainland. Early writers who ventured to the Cape used words like bare, exposed and stormy to describe its situation – this point at which the North Minch and the North Atlantic join forces to bombard a line of cliffs. 'Wrath' is from the Norse *hvarf*, meaning 'turning point'. Norse sea-rovers altered course to sail south to the Hebrides.

What restrains the day-tripper to the Cape is the Kyle of Durness. When the tide has drained from it, a huge area of sand and mud is exposed. The flow tide creates a protective moat. I scanned a picture of northern Scotland that had been taken from a satellite, some 500 miles above the earth. At the moment the photograph was taken, the tide was out; the Kyle appeared as just a continuation of the land. Shepherds and their dogs who tend the special Sutherland type of Cheviot cross the river far to the south when rounding them up. They enter an area that few people know: an area with mile after mile of featureless walking, where the stems of ling whip the ankles and where bogs threaten to tear the boots from a walker's feet.

I waited near the Cape Wrath Hotel for the small, white-painted ferry boat, with outboard engine attached, that voyages confidently at flow tide, picks its way around sandbanks at half-tide and is laid up at the ebb. It was natural to wonder how a mini-bus I saw on the opposite bank had been taken across the water; it was conveyed on a special raft. The ferryman's wife, who was waiting near the hotel, told me she had not seen her husband for several days and that rough water had kept them apart on the day of their silver wedding anniversary.

Viewed from Keoldale, the wooded shore of the Cape Wrath peninsula, a mere half mile away, belied the appearance of the wild country beyond. A sheep eyed my rucksack. Seals hauled themselves onto the sandbanks or simply waited for the tide to maroon them. Rumour had it that units of the Royal Navy were in the area, for part of the peninsula is a bombardment range. A notice expressed it forcibly: 'It is dangerous to stray from the road or to enter this area owing to unexploded shells.' Long before the Norse skippers turned their clinker-built craft for the run to the Hebrides, Roman galleys turned at Cape Wrath, and it seems that their masters were disinclined to land on such a wild shore. The Gaelic word *parph* referred to a large area, 'an excellent and delectable place for hunting'. Red deer abounded, and sometimes they were driven into the Ocean Sea (Atlantic) at the Pharohead (Cape Wrath), 'where they take them in Boats as they list'. The opening of the Caledonian Canal in 1822 was welcomed by mariners who no longer needed to make the dangerous voyage through the Pentland Firth and round the Cape. The crofter-fishermen of the locality sailed their boats into the Minch for cod or near to the cliffs of the Cape for ling.

There is a long, rough walk to Cape Wrath from the south. For some, it is the only way to visit this north-western extremity of Scotland, with its sweeping bay at Sandwood, cliffs soaring to a height of 400 feet, and a view of lonely stacks such as Am Buachaille, 'the herdsman', which attains a height of 220 feet. Skuas have colonized the wilderness; a walker, following the sheep-trods and fording the rivers, is likely to have at least one bonxie screaming about his ears.

Taking the easy route, I stepped into the ferryboat and undertook the brief voyage, in the company of eiders that were towing rafts of downy young. The ferryman's house, which from a distance had been a white blob, was now seen to have red in its colour scheme; the road beyond took an upward slant, meandering until it could straighten out above the Kyle. The road had a hard surface, but no road-roller had been here. I heard that roadmen using the ferryboat had developed the art of pouring tar in the hollows and adding a quota of stone.

The road is eleven miles long, terminating with the famous lighthouse. A visitor of 1925 wrote of the 'utter loneliness of the approach', which she contrasted with the bustle of men at the lighthouse. On my first visit, our mini-bus had splashed through the Daill Ford with the driver relating that someone had run over a salmon. It was surely the first salmon road-victim in Britain. In the summer of 1981, the Royal Engineers made a repeat of this little tragedy unlikely by constructing a Bailey bridge with a hundred-feet double span, the materials being provided by the Lighthouse Board and the Highlands Regional Council.

Telegraph poles that kept the road close company seemed shorter than usual; perhaps they were determined to keep their heads down where the Fleet lobs shells. The targets are set on Beinn Aniduibhe and Garvie Island. I heard of the stray shell that grazed a gate before burying itself in peat. Not surprisingly, the gate had not opened smoothly since that date. The Navy acknowledged its debt to the people of the district in the autumn of 1980, when helicopters removed derelict cars from around Durness, lifting them to the range, where they served as targets.

Where the Lewisian gneiss has its final grand flourish, a lighthouse was built by Robert Stevenson and his family, who on their annual inspection voyages, in August, had many stormy days off Cape Wrath. In 1798, Stevenson's gale-tossed ship lost part of its rigging, and he was obliged to bear away. 'The wind got to such a height that we were afraid to keep out longer in case she should be carried past the Orkneys altogether, and so have no harbour to leeward. We therefore put about, and on 20th August came into Stromness harbour.' That storm lasted for over a fortnight.

During another inspection tour, the main boom was carried away. David, the master builder's son – a passenger in 1830 – remembered Cape Wrath because the 'sea was running mountains high and, dashing against the rocks, sent the spray and foam far over the land'. The Stevensons had their revenge on the sea demons by constructing the lighthouse. When the lamp was delivered, calm conditions prevailed. A service was held on the ship during the Sabbath. 'The stars seemed to be infinitely numerous, and the waters of the sea on fire with phosphorescent appearance where it impinged or dashed against the vessel. After we had gone to bed, we were called up on deck to see the singular appearance of the moon in the south-east. The aurora borealis also formed a splendid semicircular zone which enlivened the whole north.'

Walter Scott, the distinguished passenger in 1814,

saw a pair of large eagles, and if I had had the rifle-gun might have had a shot, for the birds, when I first saw them, were perched on a rock within about sixty or seventy yards. They are, I suppose, little disturbed here for they showed no great alarm. . . . Mr Stevenson has fixed on an advantageous situation. It is a high promontory, with steep sides that go sheer down to the breakers, which lash its feet. There is no landing, except in a small creek about a mile and a half to the eastward. There the foam of the sea plays at long bowls with a huge collection of large stones, some of them a ton in weight, but which these fearful billows chuck up and down as a child tosses a ball. The walk from thence to the cape was over rough boggy ground, but good sheep pasture.

Cape Wrath was to Scott 'this dead Cape'. He did acknowledge its striking appearance and 'the mental association of its being the extreme Cape in Scotland, with reference to the north-west. There is no land in the direct line between this point and America.' My interest was in the Torridonian sandstone, a mile or two eastwards of the Cape, where the large seabird colonies are to be found. I followed a path to Kervaig, a delightful cove. The sheep I saw were undoubtedly the descendants of those which Scott had observed in the early part of last century. In his day, the proprietor intended to evict the crofters to make room for more sheep.

A tumult of foam-crested waves, backed by a wind coming straight from the Arctic, with no intermediate land to slow it down, provided a spectacular show under a blue sky. A bonxie tugged at something on the beach, took to the air half-heartedly, changed its mind and returned to the object of its interest. Thrift, stonecrop and rose-root decked the rocks on which I sat. The lighthouse demanded to be noticed, perched 370 feet above the sea, with a view – in calm conditions – of North Rona, the Butt of Lewis and the island of Harris. The Orkneys smudge the skyline to the north.

Through binoculars I watched the gannets that commuted between their nesting islands and the places where fish were shoaling. The rusty form of an oil-tanker sent a chill down my spine at the thought of an accidental spillage of oil. I was on a coastline of superlatives, featuring Cleit Dubh (850 feet), the highest cliff on the British mainland, and Clo Mor (600 feet), offering abundant ledges, nooks and crannies to a diverse community of birds. There is soil, too, in which the puffins can burrow. D. Nethersole-Thompson, who knows the birdlife of Scotland as well as any man, considers that 'for sheer size, clamour and excitement, Clo Mor is supreme among Scottish mainland bird cliffs.'

The cliff path led me through a pink-and-green environment: the pink of sandstone, the green of grass, which was surprisingly extensive and lush, extending to the sheer bird-whitened cliffs immediately above the sea. A promontory of pink rock was a high perch for razorbills and puffins. The grassier stretches, awesome in their setting, were intensively colonised by puffins, and I could not imagine anyone wishing to visit them.

The glory of Clo Mor must be most evident when viewed from a boat cruising between the terrifying verticals of the mainland and the several huge stacks that are as arresting as pieces of modern sculpture. Remnants of a former coastline, smoothed by many tides, daubed white by guillemots, these stacks rose in tiers of broad ledges, reminding me of iced wedding-cakes!

Guillemots had the numerical superiority. Some of the largest guillemot colonies in Britain are situated on the cliffs and stacks between Handa and the western coastline of Orkney. It is guess-timated that over 20,000 pairs frequent Clo Mor. Being a trusting soul, I will not dispute this figure.

Photographs of guillemots on a ledge fix the image in such a way that the novice cannot visualise the ceaseless noise and bustle. Some guillemots stand as erect as guardsmen, and others have assumed a half-crouching posture, facing away from the sea, with eggs pressed against their brood patches. Guillemots bob and wave their heads. A new arrival, pushing its way into the throng, opens its black beak to reveal a bright orange gape. A stranger arrives and is repulsed by a jab from a beak that sends it over the edge into a steep glide until the whirring wings give it the power of controlled motion.

From the tenements of the guillemot colony rise waves of raucous sound. Through numberless generations, these auks have adapted themselves to a nesting routine carried out on precarious, wind-swept ledges, where eggs or young may be only a foot or so from destruction. So great is the competition for the best ledges that the first guillemots are back from the sea in early January, months before the eggs will be laid. The pressure increases with the spread of other cliff-nesting species: gannet and fulmar.

Early in the season, the quarrelsome birds stake their claims. Those first arrivals, few in number, may remain on the ledges for just a few hours, at first light, their presence or absence being as erratic as the weather patterns and the movement of the fish shoals. Wintering fish are neither as plentiful nor as predictable in their movements as they are during the spring or summer. Male and female guillemots look alike and while courting express their feelings through voice and manner. A pair-bond between adjacent birds is established through bill-touching and mutual preening.

Guillemots copulate on the ledges; there is no nest as such, the large pyriform egg being laid on solid rock. Happily for the guillemot, the guano which it so plentifully distributed about the ledges provides a non-skid surface which in some cases prevents the eggs from tumbling off, and in any case the egg's distinctive shape means that when disturbed it tends to move in a circle. Some guillemots, panicked into flight, may not have sufficient time to disengage the eggs from the brood-patches, and they tumble onto the rocks far below. If an egg has not been incubated for long, it will be replaced. One patient observer of guillemots noted that the well-set egg needs less room in which to revolve. Its centre of gravity has shifted towards the narrow end!

I have mentioned the attractive appearance of the guillemot egg. Onto a ground tint of pale green or blue there is laid a variety of squiggles and blotches. There is a theory that a guillemot can recognise its egg by sight alone. A friend asserts that a guillemot simply covers the nearest egg! The guillemot may have a protracted courtship period, but little time is lost in getting the chick to sea, where it might be near to the fishing grounds. The egg hatches; the downy chick is lively and strong from that moment, and it has the strength in its feet to enable it to cling if there is a risk of it being pushed over the edge. It avoids becoming cold and wet in a heavy shower by slipping under the wing of an adult, which adopts a crouching stance. Guillemot evolution now decrees that within days the feathers begin to form. Soon the restless chick is exercising its stubby wings. The down has been replaced by a feathery suit which is quite waterproof.

Comes the moment of departure from the land. The chick is by no means fully grown. At dusk, in July, the calling of adult birds and the *peeping* of the young birds join in a strange medley of primeval sound, complemented by the boom of the waves. The chick is encouraged to leap. Tiny bodies make a fluttering descent to rock or water; the birds that alight on rocks are soon up and about, making for the sea. Adults and young paddle away from land. The adults take the opportunity to moult, and the chicks, though able to swim and dive, are not yet able to fly. The families move eastwards, loitering in areas of good fishing. It is at this time that they are specially vulnerable to oil-slicks.

After the heady experience of walking by the sea, in the company of thousands of birds, I entered the silent wilderness of the moors, my feet muffled by peat or sphagnum. The moor was tonally dead under heavy cloud, except where cotton grass picked up every available glimmer and reflected it round about. The whistle of a golden plover, low and sad, came from a bird perched, bottle-shaped, on a cushion of heather. The golden plover is a distinctive bird of the moors, of the heather, its British distribution being virtually the same as the red grouse. It is a bird of well-managed moors, where the heather does not become rank; hatching off its chicks, it takes them to the boggy areas where they can feed on insects.

Sundown was a fantasy of light and colour. Not until 11.30 p.m. did the red orb of the sun tickle the horizon. Meanwhile, in its downward progress, it tinted a belt of cloud, which became purply red. I looked for the green flash that is said to follow the final disappearance of the sun, and – disappointed – I turned away. Then various objects took on a green hue. The strangest was a light-green gull!

# 10

# Shetland: Land of the Simmer Dim

It was an uneasy dawn, with light seeping into a moist world. Layers of cloud, in various shades of grey, were like washes applied by an energetic water-colourist. The *St Clair*, over ten hours out of Aberdeen, had spent the brief night flirting with a north-easterly swell, a persistent wind blowing around an anti-cyclone centred on Scandinavia.

The view from my cabin was of a grey sky and a mass of heaving water. A fulmar, our northern albatross, glided by – *into* the wind – and I fancied that it gave me a wink before soaring from a trough, neatly avoiding a cascade of spume. I was close to Shetland and 'da simmer dim', which George Scott-Moncrieff called 'the darkless Shetland summer night'. At midsummer, if the sky is clear, the sun may be visible for almost nineteen hours, and the rest of the day is a bright twilight or, with cloud cover, a murky interlude between two long days. The 'simmer dim' is the next best thing to a Midnight Sun.

Bird-watchers, with beards and binoculars, were already on deck. A young man scanned the salty wastes for kittiwakes. He was on his first visit to Scotland, and he half-expected to find icebergs trundling along the seabed off Shetland. The lad's destination was Fair Isle, which we had passed in the night. He planned to approach the island from the north, as a passenger in the *Good Shepherd*. I did not mention the fierce ocean current, the Sumburgh Roost, which produces a lively sea in the area where the *Good Shepherd* operates.

The visitor found his kittiwakes. A stray beam of light picked out a score of birds as they rested on the tossing sea. He became lyrical as he described the kittiwakes: ocean birds with 'their big white heads, and eyes set in them like black gems'. A Dutch ornithologist whose special interest was in counting migratory seabirds was now about to observe many of them in their northern nesting haunts. The fulmar captivated him. 'Wizzout beating ze wings, he goes faster than ze boat – against ze prevailing wind,' he says, with much feeling.

A lighthouseman from Bressay, returning to his station after a long leave, was amused to hear me call the sea 'rough'. He regaled me with stories of waves breaking over the summits of lighthouses on remote islands. He told me some stories of Orkney, mentioning North Ronaldsay, the most northerly island in that group, a fertile plot ringed, at high-water mark, by a substantial wall, devised to keep the seaweed-eating sheep from entering the best land!

Walter Scott experienced a storm as he sailed for Shetland on his round of the Northern Lights. 'The breeze increases – weather may be called rough; worse and worse after we are in our berths, nothing but booming, trampling and whizzing of waves about our ears, and ever and anon, as we fall asleep, our ribs come in contact with those of the vessel . . .'

North of Dunnet Head, which is the most northerly point on the British mainland, the weather is a never-ending topic. The Shetland climate, like the ways of the Shetlanders, is not inclined towards extremes. Normally, a mildish summer is followed by a mildish winter, yet within the past twelve months – said an islander who joined us at the ship's rail – there *had* been extremes. Before Christmas, he had walked on snow that was so dry it squeaked under his feet. Less than a fortnight before I met him, he had seen a bikini-clad girl helping with the 'peats'.

It's the wind that numbs the brain. The wind sweeps across a virtually treeless landscape, gusting in a way that rattles the roofing slates. On a February day in 1962, a gust of over 177 m.p.h. was recorded at the top of Saxa Vord, on the north coast of Unst. Then the anemometer blew away! The rain tends to be persistent rather than torrential. There's a summer mist, the *haar*, which is yet another Norse term. An early writer about the northern isles mentioned 'the vapour of the sea [that] tempers the air'.

I shared a table in the cafeteria with a wise old Shetlander who smiled when I told him of warning that I must never refer to the 'Shetlands'; it must be Shetland or the Shetland Isles. He mischievously suggested that I say 'Shetlands' and explain that I was distinguishing between the northern and southern groups of islands!

The escorting gulls left us sometime during the night. We now had the company of 'bonxies', dark brown buccaneers, fast and agile enough to fly down almost any seabird and harass it until the victim parted with its latest meal (an art which has the unlovely name of kleptoparasitism). The nearest skua dived low, showing off the white triangles on its brown wings. Half of the British nesting population of great skuas, some 5,000 pairs, is to be found in Shetland, where the nickname 'bonxie' originally described a thick-set person.

The skua maintained its station with scarcely a wingbeat; it veered to the left, then right, then left again, as though keeping its eyes on the ornithologists who clustered on the after-deck. Most of them regarded the skua with a scientific detachment, but one became 'het up' about the bird's depredations – the way it victimised puffins, kittiwakes and gannets. (I mused on what man had done to birds. On Unst, puffins were dragged from their burrows using a stick with a sharp hook on one end. On Yell, seafowl were caught using a hook and line deployed from the clifftops. On Foula, and many other places, men descended cliff faces using ropes and mercilessly removed eggs or adult birds.)

Two bonxies hung about a flock of herring-gulls at the stern of a local trawler. Why squabble for food when it could so easily be taken from the bird that had initially grabbed it in the fray? John Brand, a Church of Scotland minister in 1701, wrote of the Arctic skua, which also has perfected the pursuit-and-harry technique: 'There is a fowl . . . which doth live upon the vomit and excrements of other Fowls whom they pursue and, having apprehended them, they cause them to Vomit up what they have lately taken and not yet digested. The Lord's Work both of Nature and Grace are wonderful, all speaking forth His Glorious Goodness, Wisdom and Power.'

The *St Clair* entered the channel between the Mainland and Bressay towards the end of a 200-mile voyage. Bard Head, on Bressay, took the attention from Foula, the 'bird island', that lay far to the west. Beyond Bressay, and yet appearing to be of the same land mass, was the wedge-shaped Isle of Noss, its eastern cliffs soaring to about 600 feet. There was endless bird traffic. Gannet, guillemot, puffin, shearwater – all were coping with the wind in their distinctive ways. One fulmar was lightly oiled on its breast. Several guillemots, having surfaced near the boat, were carried high on a wave. As that wave broke, they beat their wings prettily to maintain their balance. An Arctic tern looked far too delicate for the conditions – and then I took into account the circumstances of its flight to and from its winter-quarters in Antarctica. The tern hovered and plunged, the accuracy of its movements being made possible by the long outer primaries of its wings.

My lighthouseman friend pointed to Mousa, an island unin-habited by man but frequented by sheep and ponies, common seals and the storm-petrel, the smallest of our British seabirds, a mere six inches long, weighing less than an ounce. It feeds while hovering over water, but the feet touch the surface. It dines on zooplankton and the smallest of fishes. For months on end, the storm-petrel ranges the oceans, and during this time – from the hatching of its egg, right through to the start of the next breeding season – the bird is in some stage of moulting, first the body, then the tail and finally the primaries and secondaries.

Mousa's attraction to the storm-petrel lies in a prehistoric broch, over forty feet high and fifteen feet at the base of the circular wall. The petrel is not unique among birds in having developed an interest in archaeology; the broch is a nesting site, for it is composed of dry stones, without a dab of mortar. The musky tang of storm-petrels hangs about the ancient structure. Throngs of chattering birds are heard at night, as birds fly in to relieve their mates at the nests.

Shetland, with its hundred islands and 2,500 freshwater lochs, its voes and low hills, over-awed even a Roman fleet. The sailors stared at 'Thule', but no more, wrote Tacitus. 'Nowhere does the sea hold wider sway; it carries to and fro in its motions a mass of currents, and in its ebb and flow it is not held by the coast but penetrates deep into the land and winds about in the hills, as if it were its own domain.'

I was a 'soothmoother', arriving in Lerwick from the south. The equivalent term in Orkney is 'ferrylouper'. For 500 years, the period of Scandinavian rule, true friends approached what is now the capital of the Shetland Isles from the north. Not until the fifteenth century was this group of islands ceded to Scotland. The *St Clair* came slowly to rest at Lerwick ('*Leir-vik*', or 'clay creek').

The big boat's arrival, and its approach to the landing place stern-on, led to a tystie going through its head-dipping routine. There were gulls, of course: herring-gulls in full cry. The tourist literature had forecast:

> Few visitors to Shetland can remain for long unaware of the island's bird life, even if it is only the wheeling, screaming hordes of gulls which follow the fishing boats into Lerwick harbour. Although most of these breed in the cliffs and on hillsides within a few miles of the town, a number of herring gulls nest on rooftops in Lerwick itself. Even if it may be annoying to be woken up at four in the morning by the sound of a nestful of gull chicks being fed only a few yards from your hotel bedroom window, this is much more the sound of Shetland than the rumble of traffic.

A replica of a Norse longboat rode high in the water. Shetlanders are proud of their Norse ancestry; the local people lose their inhibitions at the mid-winter festival of Up-Helly-Aa, during which a carefully constructed longboat is consumed by the fire of torches thrown into it. At the most recent festivity, two early patients at Lerwick hospital were Prince Charming, with 'glitter' in his eyes, and a man whose only apparel was a single outfit designed to make him look like a bear. This bear had a sore toe!

I drove off the *St Clair*, travelled for a short distance down the road and drove aboard the red, white and blue ferry that operates between Mainland and Bressay, a half-mile journey. I heard my first tale of the sea. A visiting skipper left Lerwick for the oil-rigs, which lay due east. He set the appropriate course. It was night when the boat departed; the skipper had forgotten about Bressay; his craft ran up the beach!

I crossed the island with an undue haste, anxious to catch the wee ferry and be taken across the sound to the Isle of Noss. I do remember the long, lean forms of divers on the lochs, and the skuas that had assembled at the water's edge to wash the salt from their plumage. A rough track headed diagonally down the hill from the car-park to the rocks from which I might board the inflatable craft that maintains a shuttle service from Bressay to Noss. An eider duck, young birds in attendance, kept a wary eye on the sky, from which might come danger in the shape of a hungry skua.

In the language of the Norse folk, 'Noss' means 'a point of rock'. It is a bare island on which – it is said – the tallest plant is the rhubarb in the garden at Gungstie, where naturalists stay and the ferry attendant is based. A stranger is charmed by the local placenames: Whiggie Geo (geo – from a Norse word meaning creek), Punsgeo and North Croo. The inlets were voes – Nesti Voe and Voe of Mels. The Papae or Pictish priests are remembered through the name Papil Geo.

A team of army engineers, given a few hours, would bridge the gap between Bressay and Noss, but I was glad that Noss had retained its island status. There is no guarantee that a visitor will be able to reach it. A northerly wind whipped the open sea into white-tops; they bore down on the channel and had the spirit taken from them by a sandbar. I was able to cross. A southerly wind drives the sea into a narrowing gap where the water is no more than six fathoms deep, and Noss becomes impregnable to anyone who does not possess a helicopter.

Visitors down the years were to remember the crossing to Noss not only for its turbulence but for the characterful nature of the boatmen. A Shetlander goes sailing almost as soon as he has the size and strength to clamber over the gunwale of a boat, but some appear to have derived quiet satisfaction from teasing tourists. To one group of visitors, the skiff was 'miserable' and the boatmen 'stupidly apathetic'. They contrived to have the boat moving in a circle 'in the midst of a boiling current, and almost equally distant from either shore!'

Shetland has a distinctive type of boat – a sixareen, which is whaler-built, with a tapered point at each end, 'so that the rudder can be hooked on either at pleasure,' wrote Walter Scott. 'These vessels look very frail, but are admirably adapted to the stormy seas, where they live when a ship's boat stiffly and compactly built must necessarily perish. They owe this to their elasticity and lightness.' Haaf-fishermen from Mainland stayed on Noss, and from here they sailed or rowed their sixareens far out to sea, looking for prime fish, which they cured and sold to the owner of the island – the sort of work which might be classified as 'blood for money'.

The inflatable boat had an outboard engine and a young woman at the controls. We zigzagged across the sound in deference to the eider families. I looked through clear water to where unseen currents stirred the tough aquatic weed. The engine beat slackened as we encountered a slight swell. The boat was tied up to a projection of rock within a few paces of Gungstie, where a starling – assuredly the Shetland form of starling – greeted me with a whistle (the Shetland sub-species is said to be larger than that nesting on the mainland of Britain).

My round-the-island walk avoided the moorland areas by request. I could see patches of cotton-grass, which is known in Shetland as 'Luckaminnie's Oo'. Bare and rolling, Noss appeared to be shadowless; the sunlight flecked the sound, beyond which – in deepest shadow – lay Bard Head. Tysties lay at anchor. Oystercatchers sounded an alarm and watched their chicks dive for cover.

At the Point of Harvie, I stood in a natural rock garden, stained by a carpet of sea pinks varied by flowers of yellow hue and by the deep red of the Shetland variety of red campion. White campion had little chance to attract attention to itself with such a floral array, especially as the rocks were painted by colourful lichen.

A drystone wall, built to restrain domestic animals at the edge of the fearsome cliffs, was now badly gapped. I chanced to look over a cliff and was spotted by one of the great black-backed gulls nesting on Cradle Holme. The bass baritone voice of the gull joined the seabird chorus, and one bird peevishly dived and, screaming, passed at a range of a few yards, its flight taking it to a knoll, where it pitched, fidgeting and fretting.

Cradle Holm is a huge detached chunk of Noss that looks impregnable except to a climber of the status of Joe Brown. The name is derived from the oblong box, 'of course workmanship, with two holes at either end', that was used with a system of ropes to transport men and sheep – also any captured seabirds and their eggs – across the gap. This method of transport was last used in 1864. The device appears to have been first used in 1600, when a man scaled the cliffs without aid, hammering in two stakes from which ropes were slung. People travelled in the box with ease if not in comfort.

Scott heard about the famous cradle, 'a sort of wooden chair, travelling from precipice to precipice on rings, which run upon two cables stretched across the gulf. We viewed this extraordinary contrivance from beneath, at the distance of perhaps one hundred fathoms at least. The boatman made light of the risk of crossing it, but it must be tremendous to a brain disposed to be giddy. Seen from beneath, a man in the basket would resemble a large crow or raven, floating between rock and rock.'

I looked through a stratum of seabirds to where shags occupied the large ledges near the sea. Against a chorus of raucous voices came a powerful soloist, the diminutive Shetland wren. Where the topmost ledge was tangled with vegetation, the head of a puffin was in view, the rest of the creature being tucked away in its nesting burrow. The motionless bird appeared to be debating with itself whether or not to fly. Tammie Norie – as the Shetlander calls the puffin – seems apprehensive, as well it might be with the great black-backed gulls nesting nearby.

We looked at each other – the puffin and I. June is perhaps the best time to approach the bird, which at other times seems wary to the point of timidity. The horny sheath of the bill was brightly banded with red, yellow and blue. From the orange-red feet protruded dark claws. The puffin, having mulled over the circumstances, decided to fly, moving on short, relatively broad wings. There was no question of gliding; it beat its wings furiously and, meanwhile, contrived to look over its shoulder, as though scared that I might be following! My last view of the puffins was of birds standing in the sunshine on the stones of the old wall. A bird preened; another arrived with a white feather clasped in its beak. The others simply stood and returned my gaze, or they assembled in little groups, as though anxious to discuss the gossip of the day.

I inched my way over a slab of sandstone, in full view of the Noup of Noss. The breeze delivered the tang of seabirds. Another inch or two, and I was looking into space – to where the sea, hundreds of feet below me, smacked its lips against cliffs that had been providentially weathered into horizontal ledges, quite broad ledges, ideal for gannets. And, indeed, gannets were in occupation – the first of over 5,000 pairs that nest on the island of Noss. Ledge after ledge had its solemn, brooding birds. Each nest was just beyond pecking range of the neighbours, and the effect was of neatness. Gannets first prospected Noss in 1911 or 1912, and the first pair bred as recently as 1914. Gannets have virtually swamped the old guillemot ledges. Rows and rows of gannets, looking chalky white in shadow, quietly pass a warm summer afternoon.

Men used to descend this cliff to take 'sea-fowl' for their feathers. A man might collect five or six dozen in an expedition. Visitors who approached by sea saw that the base of the cliffs abounded with caverns. Walter Scott was taken into a cave known as the Orkney-man's Harbour, because an Orkney vessel had run in to it some years before to escape a French privateer. 'The entrance was lofty enough to admit us without striking the mast, but a sudden turn in the direction of the cave would have consigned us to utter darkness if we had gone in further. The droppings of the sea-fowl and cormorants into the water from the sides of the cavern, when disturbed by our approach, had something in it wild and terrible.'

Birds abounded on the grassy slopes on the seaward side of the Noup. This was a vantage-point not only for the bird-busy sea but for the isles of Shetland: a panorama of humps of land with their attendant sounds and voes, of rock and sea. I re-discovered the coastal path and jog-trotted towards the ferry. Bonxies reclined on the moor. The ground was littered with their victims: with the feathers and dry bones of kittiwakes and even gannets. George Scott-Moncrieff met the skuas of Noss. 'As one comes into each nesting preserve, the bonxie lifts itself with an indignant noise like crunching gravel, poises, draws back its wings, and plunges at one's head, customarily just missing it. . . .'

I went to Noss on a day when there were six human visitors. As I left the ferry and climbed back towards the Bressay car-park, I looked back to see wavering lines of birds on the calm sea. Eiders, mainly drakes, were paddling back to the shore.

# 11

# Shetland:
# The Ubiquitous Mallie

When sleep eluded me, I counted fulmars, which are far more common than sheep. Maalie, the old Shetland name, is derived from *foul maa* – the gull that smells! A fulmar is not a gull, of course, but a petrel, and unlike most other species of petrel it nests on an open cliff and can be seen lolling about or brooding its egg during the day. Shetland has a profusion of fulmars. The tourist literature hints at the bird's common status: 'And everywhere the fulmars, wheeling and gliding silently or raucously chattering in almost every possible niche; they treat other birds, and even man, with indifference.'

You will recall that the fulmar was the first bird I saw in Shetland waters. On Noss, the fulmar was not only wheeling and gliding but occupying every suitable ledge and crevice on the low cliffs and also nesting on the moorland. The first fulmars were seen on Noss just before the end of last century; by 1946 there were some 1,000 pairs and the figure is now well over 5,000 pairs.

A fulmar on a ledge looks to be at peace with the world. It sits for long periods, apparently dozing. Approach it, and there is no immediate response. The head remains sunk into the body, and the bird fixes you with its dark eyes. Take two more paces, and if the fulmar is a young bird that is simply holding a territory at which it will nest another year, it stumbles away on its short legs, tumbling over the cliff edge to float gracefully on the rising air. A fulmar with a hard-set egg beneath it becomes agitated, as well it might. It works the muscles of its throat, partly opens its wings and is restlessly alert. Advance a little further, and it will send a jet of oil from its stomach in your direction.

The stocky, thick-plumaged fulmar at the southern end of its vast range is a pale-looking bird. The shades are so pale, indeed, you wonder if the bird has been over-exposed to the bleaching effects of the sun. Silver-grey is the tone of its back and the upper sides of its wings. The body is white, with a yellow tinge. The beak, with its various pastel shades, will claim your attention. It is a heavy beak, tipped with a hook. Large tubular nostrils are set on the upper mandible. The Antarctic may have been the cradle of this now-familiar species, but it has lived in the North Atlantic long enough for two main forms to appear: the so-called 'blue' form and the light form. The dark, short-billed fulmar is a bird of the high Arctic, where it revels in the power of the wind over a cold sea that is nonetheless rich in planktonic crustacea. The light form is the one nesting around Britain, and it has a larger bill than its northern cousin. There are intermediate forms.

Shetland has become virtually one large fulmar colony. The bird is heard cackling all the way from Muckle Flugga to Fair Isle. One fulmar skimmed the road just ahead of my car; others were to be seen patrolling the sounds between the isles, and I found pairs nesting on newly cut rock just behind a toilet block at the Unst ferry landing. While on Unst, I heard the fulmar cackle from grassy ledges high above Northwick. Fulmars rested, with withdrawn undercarriages, on the road to Skaw, Britain's most northerly house. At Hermaness and other large seabird resorts, fulmars were on constant patrol, gliding or hanging on the wind, tails widespread, grey-webbed feet trailing. (There had been five sitting birds on a ledge immediately below my main vantage-point near the Noup of Noss.)

The bird literature is full of fine passages that extol the bird's flying ability at sea. 'They are strong and graceful on the wing,' wrote R. A. Goodsir, 'flying almost in the teeth of the strongest gale, without any seeming movement of their beautifully-rounded pinions; now swooping along in the troughs of the sea, now skimming on the snowy crests. They are almost constantly on the wing, night and day, never alighting on the water, except during calm and moderate weather, and then but rarely.'

For centuries, the St Kildans were the only Britons who saw the fulmar; they ate the bird with a relish we associate with chicken or turkey. Each islander consumed over a hundred fulmars a year, and the cull was controlled in the interests of future food supplies. By taking the fulmars, the St Kildans did not permit the colony to grow appreciably, yielding surplus birds that might colonise other areas. The fulmars that arrived in Shetland, and subsequently spread to many points on the British coastline, were from the Faroes.

Ornithologists have debated hard and long about the astonishing spread of the fulmar. Changes in the food supply appear to be significant. Perhaps the fulmars that appeared off Shetland over a thousand years ago were attracted by man's fishing activities. The bones of fulmars were found in the rubbish heaps of Jarlshof, on Mainland. Maybe the fulmars were hooked on the long lines that Viking fishermen paid out to catch cod or ling, or the eagerness of the birds to share the feast brought them within clubbing distance of the men.

James Fisher referred to the 'astonishing eagerness' with which fulmars attended the flensing of a whale or the skinning of a seal. When a school of whales ran onto the beach in Uyea sound, on Unst, in the autumn of 1805, fulmars were among the scavengers, and the birds stayed all winter, gorging themselves on the rotting carcasses. Then, in the summer of 1891, a dead whale was washed up on the island of Foula. The attendant fulmars stayed to breed on the dizzying heights of The Kame (1,220 feet).

William Scoresby junior, a Yorkshire whaling skipper who was familiar with Arctic waters, wrote that fulmars 'are extremely greedy of the fat of the whale' and 'though few should be seen when a whale is about to be captured, yet, as soon as the flensing process commences, they rush in from all quarters, and frequently accumulate to many thousands in number. They then occupy the greasy track of the ship; and, being audaciously greedy, fearlessly advance within a few yards of the men employed in cutting up the whale.' Fulmars attacking the fat came within clubbing distance of the men and were 'knocked down with boat-hooks, in great numbers, and sometimes taken up by the hand'.

Scoresby mentioned the alarm as thousands of fulmars took flight; the way the birds 'assist their wings, for the first few yards, by striking the water with their feet'. He observed the voracity with which they grabbed pieces of fat, 'the curious chuckling noise which, in their anxiety for dispatch, they always make', and their gluttony, which often meant they were unable to fly and must clamber onto the nearest piece of ice, 'where they rest until the advancement of digestion restores their wonted powers. Then, if opportunity admit, they return with the same guest to the banquet as before: and, though numbers of the species may be killed, and allowed to float about among them, they appear unconscious of danger to themselves.'

Did the dead whale bring the first nesting fulmars to Shetland? It is the type of story that often colours folklore. James Fisher, with the help of Shetland naturalists, pieced together an account of the spread – from Foula, 'round the top and down', taking in headlands first, firths later, then inland sites. It began in the 1890s and revealed that the Atlantic white-phase fulmar is resourceful as well as vigorous.

I found pleasure in seeking out some of the more unusual nesting sites: a ruined crofting house, open moorland, peat workings, the foot of a drystone wall and, on Fetlar, in the cro's, those remarkable enclosures in which Shetlanders planted vegetables, away from the bite of the wind. Each cro I saw had its sentinel fulmar; each had a nesting bird within, a bird that was startled as my head appeared over the rim. The fulmar would ease itself from the nest, partly open its wings, squirm and gulp, preparing to release a jet of oil if my unwelcome attentions persisted. The mate glided backwards and forwards, at no great distance, but without a sound and showing not the slightest inclination to be aggressive. In similar circumstances, a gull would have screamed and dived, and a bonxie would have yelled and descended to slap my ears!

Victorian and Edwardian naturalists were fascinated by the fulmar, first on St Kilda, then on Shetland. Edmund Selous, who was here in 1902, watched a pair of fulmars displaying, They lay near to each other on a ledge, and 'every few minutes open their bills to the very widest extent, at the same time bowing and swelling out the skin of the throat, including that which lies between the two sides of the lower mandible, until it has a very inflated appearance. In this state they stretch their heads towards each other, and then, with languishing gestures and expression, keep moving them about from side to side, uttering while they do so, but by no means always, a hoarse, unlovely sort of note, like a series of hoarse coughs or grunts. . . .'

Harvie-Brown, visiting Rona, crept on hands and knees to the edge of a cliff on which a fulmar had been observed. He craned over to get a better view of the face; and 'my delight was great when I saw a Fulmar sitting, apparently on its nest. . . . Wishing to see if she was breeding, I threw down several small stones and, not without some trouble, managed at last to dislodge her. My disappointment was as great as my previous delight, when I saw an empty nest.'

In 1897, as the fulmar swept around the northern isles, the Keartons were on St Kilda, thrilled at meeting a species that had for so long had its only British nesting haunts on these remote islands. Cherry Kearton, the athletic brother, followed a ledge for some distance, 'and then carefully working his way down crevices, with his face to the cliff and his camera held by a strap which he gripped firmly betwixt his teeth – much in the same way a fox is said to carry a heavy goose to his lair – he got near to one bird'. The fulmar spat!

> When he got pretty close up to her [wrote Richard Kearton], I saw the fulmar squirt a quantity of amber-coloured oil at him. It travelled three or four feet, describing a kind of half-circle and falling short of the mark. . . . As the photographer got nearer and commenced to fix up his apparatus amongst some huge boulders, I noticed the bird moving her head and neck rapidly up and down as if trying to remove some obstacle from her throat. In less than two minutes she again ejected a quantity of oil, and as my brother had actually crept within a yard of her, with much greater precision and effect. Some of the oil landed on the jacket-sleeve of his right arm.

This spitting, a defensive ploy, has proved to be singularly effective during the bird's spread. Other species, like herring-gulls, tend to give way before it, and on Noss fulmar numbers have risen sharply, while the population of herring-gulls has declined. As already related, a sea eagle introduced to Fair Isle had its plumage spattered by fulmar oil, and kittiwakes are among the sufferers, the oil apparently removing from their feathers the vital waterproofing quality. James Fisher mentioned several normal purposes for the existence of the oil. It is, for example, mixed with regurgitated food as the young are being fed. 'Whatever the origin of oil-ejection, there is no doubt about the result,' he wrote.

> It takes an experienced fulmar-addict to face a battery of incubating birds, or three-week young on the ledges of a colony. I have watched confident young men, ringing young fulmars on the steep cliffs of St

Kilda, driven into dangerous and exposed positions by the mere threat of warm oil; and I have had myself to develop a technique of counter-aggression, of swift stretch and snatch to catch the young one's necks and direct their vomit aside.

The first breeding record for Fair Isle was in 1903, and by 1959 the fulmar population had risen to 5,000 pairs. In 1969 three times that number of birds nested along the coast. The growth rate has slowed. Reports from the bird observatory on Fair Isle remark that fulmars are now absent only during severe weather in winter. In the early years of this colony, the birds had dispersed by mid-September, and they did not return until the start of the following year. In the early 1950s, they were absent from the cliffs for a few weeks in autumn, and now you can usually rely on seeing fulmars on the cliffs whatever the time of year.

A key to the fulmar's success is its longevity. This bird matures slowly and attains a breeding age at seven or eight years. During the long apprenticeship, it has become well versed in the art of survival. There has been time to prospect for a nesting site. Then the fulmar might live for over twenty years. Longevity, and an adequate food supply, must go a long way towards explaining the fulmar's success, for a nesting bird lays only one egg, and should that egg be destroyed, it will not be replaced again that season.

The nesting season is protracted. The birds return early to the selected cliff and may spend a week or two at sea, feeding without interruption, before the egg is laid. The egg is deposited on bare rock or in some soft hollow among the cliffside vegetation. Some fifty days elapse before the young bird hatches out and, covered with white down, resembles a powder-puff.

After seven weeks of good feeding, the young bird weighs more than an adult. It has shed its down and has emerged into the world with a smart plumage that differs from the adult's simply in its brightness, being white as compared to ivory. The youngster departs from the cliffs, to spend the next few years on the wide Atlantic. James Fisher wrote:

What I do not think has been fully grasped in ornithological circles is the fact that the fulmar can reach, and does reach, the middle of each ocean, because it has become a sailing-vessel, a sailplane. . . . It seems to be a fair and truthful thing to say that, given a wind of Force 4 or 5 or more on the Beaufort scale, a fulmar can get anywhere it wants without much effort.

A sailplane enthusiast, Walter Newmark, watched fulmars at Tiree and wrote about the fulmar's reliance for fore and aft stability on a very highly developed tail: 'The tail muscles are extraordinarily strong and well developed, capable of warping the tail up on one side and down on the other, and at the same time twisting the whole assembly and thus putting on bank without using aileron control.'

Shetland is now one gigantic fulmar colony. In less than a century, the 'gull' with the musky odour has made the Scottish coastline its own.

# 12

# Isle of Unst:
# The Farthest North

Wind and rain, mist and scudding cloud: they are attracted to the low, rounded hills of Shetland. From the air, some islands appear to be 50/50 land and water. When the Pleistocene ice melted, the level of the sea rose, creating a deeply indented coastline. The main airport has water on three sides; a bay to the west, a voe to the south and a 'pool' to the east. Waterfowl swim within a short distance of the runway. At nearby Fitful Head, a peregrine falcon hangs on the wind where the sea breaks against an eminence of 900 feet.

At Scalloway, a castle rises about the hubbub of a lively fishing village. Glaucous and Iceland gulls join the throng of birds scrambling for fish scraps as the boats come in on a winter day. A few pairs of long-eared owls nest among the heather on a nearby hillside, and birds sometimes roost in local gardens.

The only road hazard I met as I drove northwards from Lerwick was a great black-backed gull that tore at a bloody corpse and gave way grudgingly as I approached. For a few moments, I thought that it did not intend to move and that gluttony would be its downfall. The highway unfolded in smooth stretches. Humps and hillsides had been shaved away. Hollows had been filled. The engineers sensibly left a strip of bare ground on either side so that sheep would not graze up to the edge of the asphalt and run the risk of being knocked down by traffic. Walter Scott was unimpressed by the Shetland type of sheep, which he described as miserable looking and hairy-legged, of all colours, 'even to sky-blue'. He had often wondered where Jacob got speckled lambs. 'I think now they must have been of Shetland stock.'

During my journey, Shetland ceased to be an assembly of dots on the map of the North Atlantic; it developed into a fascinating complex of hills and moors, lochs and voes. North Mainland, which is attached to the main island by a sliver of ground, Mavis

Grind, is dominated by Ronas Hill – at 1,475 feet the highest point in Shetland. Red-throated divers and skuas rarely have their nesting haunts violated by humans. The dunlin, a lover of wet ground with some standing water, utters a trill that has a gossamer fineness, and another typical moorland species, the merlin, pursues the commonest of the upland birds, the meadow pipit. Parties of great northern divers that winter in Ronas Voe depart for their far-northern breeding grounds, leaving Shetland to the redthroat and its eerie wailing. The most northerly area, the Point of Fethaland, is like a finger indicating the position of Gruney and the Ramna Stacks, a reserve of the RSPB, where auks and kittiwakes cling to rocks that are scoured by fierce tidal currents. Esha Ness fronts the ocean with impressive cliffs, and big gulls festoon the stacks. Kittiwakes nest in abundance.

The names given to the stacks of Shetland are quaint to 'sooth-moothers', and while waiting for the ferry to Yell I glanced at the map and chuckled over some of the titles of stacks and islets that are scattered, like pieces of an unwanted jigsaw, all the way from Mainland, and south of Whalsay, to the Out Skerries. I located Hoo Stack, The Sneckson, Litla Billan, Muckle Fladdicap and Rumble, names that charmed me by their quaint unfamiliarity. A flotilla of islets near Whalsay had further improbable names: Trota Stack, Nista, Mooa and Ibister Holme. The Out Skerries themselves had gathered around them Short and Long Guen, Swaba Stack and Billia Skerry.

The Shetland folk were characterful, being originals in thought and action. There was the middle-aged Scalloway man, setting out on his motor cycle for a day trip to Fetlar, an island he had never visited. A health visitor told me that she planned to go south for her holidays – south, in the Shetland context, being Edinburgh. The sun appeared from behind cloud, as though checking that Shetland was where it should be. Shetland folk, I heard, sunbathe wearing their jumpers, with the sleeves rolled up! A boy from the school on Unst – where it would not take you long to count the trees – returned from a trip to London. Asked what he thought of the Capital, he replied: 'It was all right, but I couldn't see anything. There was too much in the way.'

Shetland is a kingdom unto itself. A village store supplied everything from cream crackers to clothes, some still bearing a wartime utility mark. Christmas decorations adorned some of the shelves – in early June. From this shop I obtained petrol and postage stamps. When I saw a plastic bag hanging from a gate, I heard that it is too windy for dustbins!

A sturdy Shetland ferry took me across Yell Sound, the playground of tidal rips. Near Tofts Voe Pier, which had been constructed in 1951, an eider and some ducklings bobbed on the short, sharp waves. A family from Lancashire planned a holiday on Yell. The husband had a permit to photograph whimbrel, though that permit did not guarantee good weather. 'It's ten-to-one that the wind will blow the hides down.'

The ferry slammed into the advancing waves, which disintegrated into sheets of spray. Salt water pattered onto the roof of the car, leaving rime on the windows. The islands – part of another RSPB reserve – came into view. Bobby Tulloch represents the RSPB on Shetland: his book on the birdlife was very informative about the islands that were now in view. I read of cave-nesting rock doves, of storm-petrels that frequent the old crofts, of Arctic terns nesting in disused fields, and skuas on the hill. Tysties frequent the sea-edge rocks. The island group supports colonies of guillemots, kittiwakes, puffins and great black-backed gulls. Common seals drop their young on quiet beaches, and grey seals pup on Gruney each autumn.

The name Yell means 'barren isle', and two-thirds of its surface is swaddled by peat. The local people do not have large fuel bills with such bounty, though peat-cutting is labour-intensive. Using wooden-handled spades called *tuskars*, pronounced 'tooshkar', the islanders slice up and expose to the sunshine and breezes the rich brown turves, which used to be moved to the crofts in panniers borne by Shetland ponies. Today the transport is a Land Rover or even a lorry, and the turves are packed into plastic bags. Coal reaches the island by boat in the summer.

My journey around Yell was invariably in the chocolate-brown landscape of the peaty moors, where I was surprised to find a large number of shalders, or oystercatchers. A small number winter on Shetland, but most of them go southwards to follow the tide in some distant estuary. This bird, bright enough on the shore, brought a carnival touch to the moors with its striking pied body, its red bill and pink legs. Before the day was out, my head rang from the shrill piping.

I found one clutch of eggs on a tussock near a peat face. The adult bird slipped from the nest and moved off with the head-down manner of the species, then rose to shout with such intensity it might have been proclaiming the end of the world. There were dozens of broods of chicks, struggling through the mini-jungle of the heather until a cry from a parent bird warned them to squat with their heads down, which they dutifully did, looking like clods of grey and buff. Oystercatchers circled. Others perched on knolls and fixed me with their red-rimmed eyes. The *kleep* of the oystercatcher is included in the repertoire of the Shetland starling, which is an accomplished mimic. The starling will also give you a snatch from the calls of whimbrel and golden plover.

The fields of mid-Yell are old-fashioned flower fields, not just acres of sappy grass, as they are when commercial strains of grass have been sown. Flowering at the roadside was the Shetland campion, of an unbelievably intense red. I watched two snipe take a zigzag course from a roadside drain. Great black-backed gulls bathed or preened in the Wick of Gossabrough, and from the hill came the vibrant trilling of a whimbrel.

A stretch of new road, between the two ferry points, had violated the nesting loch of a pair of red-throated divers. Rubble from the road workings extended into the water, which it domi-nated with a wall of raw boulders. A diver, cruising on what was left, cheerfully disregarded the passing traffic. In exceptionally wet seasons, nests are flooded and the eggs float away; in a dry season, such as this, a lochan can shrink until there is scarcely enough water to be worthy of the name 'lochan'. A diver cannot alight on land, nor can it take off from a hard surface; without water, it is virtually helpless.

Ralph Chislett left a record of a journey from water's edge to the nest that was undertaken with painful slowness by a Highland redthroat. The distance may be no more than two feet but demands much effort. To Chislett it was 'this most miserable march', the bird hobbling, its body scarcely clear of the ground. 'The efforts of an amputated man could scarcely have looked more awkward. When at length the bird reached the second flattened patch of herbage holding the eggs, she fell forward, rested for a second, shuffled half round and rested again, turned to face the water and rested again, before finally arranging her feet and the eggs to her liking. Thereafter, the bird made no movement for a couple of hours except of the head and neck.'

While waiting for ferry-time – the craft would take me to Unst – I watched a gentle-mannered Shetland farmer taking the wool from one of his best rams, a Morrit or 'moorit', of brown colouration. This man was plucking off the wool in the traditional way, which is known as 'rooin'. Shetland sheep moult their old fleeces readily, and plucking is not painful to them, though in 1619 the Scottish Privy Council considered that 'rooin' was 'grievous and noisome to the poor harmless beasts' and forbade the occupation. The islanders objected and put up such a good case for the custom to be retained that they were allowed to continue in the time-honoured way.

Shetland sheep come in a variety of shades, as Walter Scott observed long years ago, and yet only about two per cent of the sheep are coloured: black, piebald or brown. The diminutive sheep are of a moorland type. A crofter told me that he sold the surplus sheep from the lowlands and kept any surplus Shetland sheep from the hill. The family ate them!

At the ferry landing-place, steel-grey waves slapped the beach. An eider – the 'dunter' of Shetland – clucked urgently as a bonxie approached, and the ducklings, like balls of black fluff, clustered round mother's tail as she led them away. Bonxies, cunning birds that they are, have been known to co-operate in collecting eider ducklings. The eiders have adopted their own form of convoy system, and several ducks will marshal the young of the area once those ducklings have reached the sea.

Standing in a 'thin' wind, as the ferry ironed out waves in Bluemill Sound, I watched strings of gannets and auks passing to and fro – either departing for or returning from the rich feeding-grounds to the east. Gannets used shallow wingbeats or they glided. The auks flew with that sense of desperation exhibited by birds which, in the evolutionary sense, are well on their way to becoming flightless. A tern hovered, twisted in flight, dived, alighted on the water with a splash and reappeared with a fish, which it bore off.

Some of the gannets located a local shoal of fish – herring, young saithe or haddock – and the ace plunge-divers of the North Atlantic treated me to an exhibition of finely controlled flight. The fish must have been just below the surface. These gannets did not need to operate from a great height; they entered the water at an oblique angle. Unsuccessful birds returned again and again. The impact of a high dive is cushioned by air sacs under the skin; the nostrils of the bird are occluded, and so they are safe from a sudden ingress of water. Surfacing birds either lumbered into flight immediately or rode on the waves, their heads and tails at a jaunty angle. Within five minutes, the excitement was over, and normal bird traffic was seen – a procession (more precisely, several processions of birds) dominated visually by the torpedo-shaped gannets with their black wingtips.

More excitement was at hand. Bonxies arrived, anxious to share the feast by harrying other seabirds, forcing them to regurgitate their last meal. A bonxie in recline looks large and blunt – clumsy, indeed – but it flies with speed and verve at the impulse of hunger. A bonxie closed on a gannet after an impress-ive dive; the gannet was near the sea. As it climbed, the skua grabbed one of its wings, and both birds fell into the sea, in a flurry of white water. When hounding a gannet, a bonxie is just as likely to grasp the tail as it is to take hold of a wing. The object is to throw its victim off balance. Gannets and bonxies are old adver-saries, and many chases are unsuccessful. When its game of aerial robbery is not rewarded, the bonxie is quite capable of scavenging for food by other means.

The Arctic skua that appeared was slimmer, more graceful than the bonxie. The flight silhouette was distinguished by pointed wings and an elongation of the central tail feathers, which gave the bird a rakish appearance. The Arctic skua makes a speciality of hounding kittiwakes, terns and puffins, and this bird dived on a squadron of fast-moving auks which scattered in panic. A puffin ditched and dived. The skua, this time unsuccessful, departed, hopping over the waves.

I have already mentioned beached whales on which immigrant fulmars dined. A passenger on the Unst ferry said that some fifty caa'ing or pilot whales had entered the sound a few years back; the creatures were coaxed to the open sea by a man in a boat. Beached whales not only die – they smell abominably! To earlier generations, whales provided a supply of protein that gave the island life a carnival atmosphere until it was eaten. Stevenson, the lighthouse-builder, saw over 150 whales lying in the bay on Unst. 'They are easily mastered,' he wrote, 'for the first that is wounded among the sounds and straits so common in the isles usually runs ashore. The rest follow the blood and, urged on by the boats behind, run ashore also. A cut with one of the long whaling knives under the back fin is usually fatal to these huge animals.'

Robert Louis Stevenson was related to the eminent lighthouse-builder. The man who became a leading literary figure visited Unst during the construction of the lighthouse on Muckle Flugga. From here he travelled to Braemar and began work on a swash-buckling yarn, *Treasure Island*, that was to become one of the world's best-known works of fiction. Though the tale is set in tropical seas, the island's shape is remarkably similar to that of Unst, which comes within 400 miles of the Arctic Circle.

Sitting on a ridge of boulders and earth, close to the ferry landing, with the cackle of fulmars as a substitute for Stevenson's parrot, I was elated at having reached a point that was 138 nautical miles north of the Scottish mainland and only 162 miles from the Norwegian coast. I was at Ultima Thule, in fact, which the Norse imagination peopled with giants and trows (trolls).

The road I followed was a new road, blustering on its way northwards, having the devil-may-care attitude of a soldier in battle. A helicopter from the airfield near Baltasound climbed steeply, gaining its operational height for a journey to the Ninian oilfield – a saintly name for an operation based on advanced technology. The oilmen wore orange immersion-suits that would virtually guarantee their survival for three hours in the choppy, chilling North Sea, in the unlikely event of the helicopter having to ditch on its eighty-mile journey.

Unst was seen to possess what Yell had lacked – variety of scene. Initially, I crossed a tract of moorland that had been sheep-trimmed, wind-blasted, until it was little more than a stubble on the landscape. Short heather is to the liking of one of Unst's bird celebrities, the whimbrel. In the crofting areas, as on Yell, were herby fields of a type I remembered from my Pennine youth, before farmers began to plough and re-seed with commer-cial strains of grass, leaving the landscape lush but merely green. The fields of Unst were decked with yellow rattle, ragged robin, eyebright, forget-me-not, orchids, marsh marigolds and that strikingly attractive Shetland red campion (*Silene dioica spp. zetlan-dicum*).

Baltasound, revealed as a bay rather than a sound, once offered a variety of craft the shelter and facilities of a fine natural harbour. At Haroldswick, where Harold Fairhair landed in 875 to add the Northern Isles to the Crown of Norway, I could play the 'most northerly' game. I posted cards at the most northerly post office. On the Sunday evening I conducted a service at the most norther-ly church, a Methodist church with manse attached, where my congregation of fifteen included two members of the Church of Scotland, two Catholics and an Anglican. There is no religious rancour in these northernmost isles.

Every other person I met told me of the tropical weather I had just missed. The peat-cutters had been perspiring, with the men stripped to the waist and some of the young women wearing next-to-nothing. A curtain of cloud was drawn across the sky, but it was never truly dark, even at midnight. I revelled in the delights of the 'simmer dim'. Some local people tended to go to bed very late and, let it be whispered, to arise rather late next morning. One inhabitant was in the habit of playing hymns on an electronic organ before going to bed. I remember hear-ing the rather sad strains drifting through the moist air in the early hours. They disturbed a few birds that were suffering from insomnia. Another islander had a bath at 1.30 a.m. and then went out to post a letter at 2 a.m. before retiring to bed.

The 'simmer dim' was vibrant with the calls of waders. Twelve species of wader nest regularly on Unst. While walking to the castle of Muness – yes, the most northerly castle in Britain! – I sensed the air trembling with bird calls, most of them sharp and shrill. The most penetrating sound came from a redshank. Cur-lews with chicks in attendance yelped their displeasure. A lap-wing's reedy call provided a background sound to the whistle of a golden plover. A sharp-featured bird, viewed against a bank of cloud, was an exhibitionist snipe, which climbed and dived, extending the outer feathers of its tail, so that these stiffened barbs vibrated in the rushing air, emitting that curious 'bleating' sound. I listened, entranced, to the trilling of the whimbrel, which Desmond Nethersole-Thompson has called 'this beautiful boreal curlew'.

The Shetland evenings diminished into watery greys and blues through which the croaking of red-throated divers could be heard. At The Westings, I saw fulmars sitting in green pockets of vegetation around some well-fleshed stacks. I came under the gaze of inquisitive seals. In a crofter's kitchen, I sat on a sofa under rows of piltocks (young saithe) that were drying in a peat-flavoured air. Catching piltocks is an occupation for the long summer evenings; the fish are salted and dried, to be kept for winter use. 'We like the salty taste,' said the crofter's wife. 'Without salt, there wouldn't be much taste!' She would store her fish in a box in the warmest bedroom, that above the kitchen fire, and in due course the fish would be cooked and eaten with boiled potatoes. Tatties and piltocks still warm the stomachs of many a Shetland family in winter.

The house was long and low. It had recently been re-roofed and whitewashed. An outbuilding was composed, as are so many in Shetland, from a large upturned boat. The sons of the household were feeding pet lambs, and the husband was awa' on the hill, attending to a tractor that broke down with the last load of peat in tow. No one complained about this. It had been a good season for the peat. The winter store of fuel had been secured with scarcely a drop of rain upon it.

The reek of peat is one of the dominant scents of Shetland. It is possible that the local people are so accustomed to it that they no longer notice it. The half-dozen peats I collected on the Northern Isles brought happiness to an emigrant who lives in northern England. In consultation with his wife, he excitedly planned when each piece would be put on the fire. The first occasion would be a birthday!

The enclosed stove is now commonplace, and so the peat fire is no longer permitted to burn continuously. There are times when it must be allowed to go out so that the stove can be cleaned. The old open hearth was a deep pit covered by a small grate. Peat ash was allowed to accumulate, and in it the last person to go to bed buried a few glowing bits of peat. Ralph Chislett knew such a hearth. 'In the morning, the still live peats are taken out, placed on the grate, and sprinkled with dry particles, which at once catch fire and ignite the larger peats built around. Thus many a cottage fire is never allowed to die out.' At The Westings, the wife told me that when she brought a peat to the house she knocked it against a stone to displace the 'hornclocks', her term for the large black beetles that are commonly found on the upland trods in summer.

This family had gathered 360 bags of peat, and each bag was capable of holding 30 large peats.

We talked about animals. The Shetland pony, which shares the common grazings with the sheep, has an average height of three feet. The sheep carry their lambs through the long, dark winter, and at lambing time the ewe may lose its offspring to a predatory bird: a skua or a great black-backed gull. When a strong lamb is following its mother on the moor, it is frequently hounded by skuas defending their nesting territories. Skua, big gull, hooded crow: these three form an unholy trinity. I heard that a pair of hooded crows was nesting in an old crofting house and that another pair had set their nest on a 'hydro pole'. Other 'whoodies' make up for the absence of suitable trees by nesting 'among lang heather'. The bonxie was described to me as 'the shark of the sky'.

The garden of this house held a row of what I had taken to be flowering broom and was, in fact, cabbage gone to seed. Only one variety grows a heart of acceptable size on the isle of Unst, and the crofter choses some of the best plants from which to gather seed. 'One year we imported some seed from Edinburgh, but the cabbages did not grow hearts.'

North of Haroldswick and the RAF station, beyond the Methodist church and the rounded bay called Nor Wick, lay the most northerly house in Britain. To reach it I crossed moorland where bonxies lay on dry knolls, and a few Arctic skuas let off their surplus nervous energy to the accompaniment of fiendish cries. The bonxies seemed languid; the Arctic skuas were restless, pursuing each other at speed, uttering their mewing calls.

Skaw was solitary, remote, about 180 miles to the north of John o' Groats. The house appeared grey-roofed, white-walled, with some liberal applications of red paint to the door and gate, and the obligatory upturned boat serving as the ample roof of an outbuilding, a boat blackened with pitch, in true Shetland style. The gold of marsh marigolds offered visual relief from the uniform green of sheep-cropped grassland. A scattering of islets lay beyond a golden beach.

Another day, heading north-westwards, I saw one of the fairest views in Shetland. The road dipped to the low ground between Loch of Cliff, which is composed of fresh water, and Burra Firth, an arm of the sea. The golfball-like radomes of the station on Saxa Vord drew the attention on one side of the Firth, being complemented on the other by a huddle of white buildings associated with the lighthouse on Muckle Flugga. The 'creep' of soil on a nearby hillside created a pronounced terraced effect. Some of the low hills were being used by golfers, who on this day had swaddled themselves in waterproofed clothing. I had to remind myself that it was June.

An American who planned to visit Hermaness looked at the sky and remarked: 'I'm sure going to take my poncho.' He strode ahead – and I did not see him again! I was engrossed by the hundreds of common orchids that stood to attention among the straggling grasses of a hillside near the lighthouse buildings. A moorland track lay beyond. I strode on typical Shetland hill ground, with peat and heather giving way at altitude to drier, grassy expanses where grew the ubiquitous tormentil.

Hermaness Hill, long famed for its skuas and its seabird city, is not a difficult hill to climb. The moorland tract holds some 1,000 pairs of bonxies and perhaps 250 pairs of Arctic skuas. The ground beyond the summit slopes gently to cliffs and stacks where seabirds congregate in their countless thousands. T. A. Coward, who visited Hermaness in 1927, wrote: 'The ledges were congested districts, the air was filled with graceful flying fowl and, as far as the eye could reach, swimmers dotted the waves.' That is not all. Off the coast of Unst are Britain's most northerly rocks, Muckle Flugga and its attendants, set in a grey sea.

On the day of my visit, Hermaness was hard and dry – dusty, indeed – after weeks of unaccustomed drought. The vegetation crackled under my feet. Skuas made the air crackle with their guttural voices. The Unst name for the skuas is *skooi*; they nest on the drier parts of the moor, and off-duty birds perch on small knolls and prominent tussocks, spattering the ground with guano so that patches of well-fertilised grass, green against the dun shades of the moor, are to be found.

The deep voice of the bonxie – *keg*, *keg* – punctuated my walk as birds wheeled, taking the upthrust of the breeze on wings with a span of 4½ feet. The bird, which weighs over three pounds and is therefore among the avian heavyweights, suddenly enters a dive and passes the head of an intruder at a range of a few inches. The first bird to dive on me used guile as well as physical strength, tending to fly towards me from the rear. A sudden 'whoosh' of displaced air was followed by another round of cackling. A friend once experienced the nerve-tingling slap of a webbed foot against his head. I carried my trusty crook, forcing the skuas to keep their distance.

The Arctic skuas wailed like tormented cats. Off-duty birds let off energy in play; they dived, soared, twisted, turned, pursuing each other with verve and a demonstration of well-controlled power, for it was all done at high speed, sometimes well clear of the ground and sometimes while brushing the heather. The moorland rang with their wailing.

Immature bonxies form 'clubs' and over a hundred birds had gathered at the side of a lochan to while away the long summer days. An older bird bathed while standing in water to the depth of its legs, dipping its head repeatedly, sending water coursing over its back. The partially open wings were beaten against the water, creating a fine spray. This bird stretched upwards, shook surplus water from its wings and flew to the shore, its feet pattering on the surface of the loch.

The northern sky clouded, and some raindrops fell to a grateful earth. Hermaness Hill seemed to cleave the storms but eventually was overwhelmed. I scurried to a wooden hut, a conspicuous object on this treeless landscape, and the timbers creaked as the storm battered its walls. The rain was passing horizontally! There has been a hut in this prime skua country since Dr L. Edmondston decided to protect the remaining bonxies, some thirty in number. In 1891, a full-time watcher was maintained and a hut provided as shelter and focal point for visitors.

Richard Kearton was on Hermaness in 1898, a time when only thirteen pairs of bonxies were breeding. The naturalist returned with his daughter in 1913, and 'we found old Henry the watcher as quietly enthusiastic as ever over the welfare of his feathered friends, and his efforts in preserving them were successful beyond expectation.' There were now over seventy pairs, and bonxies were settling on other islands. Incidentally, that summer of 1898 was exceptional for herrings. Richard and Cherry Kearton found herring lying, 'mostly headless, in extravagant numbers round great skua nests containing young ones'. Herrings were scarce in 1913, and 'the birds were feeding their chicks on offal.'

Henry, the watcher, fed scone from his lunch pack to a pair of Arctic skuas which had nested for years within a hundred yards of the hut. (There was a pair close by at the time of my visit.) 'Whenever he showed himself, one or the other of the birds came wheeling round, and was generally rewarded by a piece of scone. They both refused [our] wholesome bread and butter, and when I smeared marmalade upon it they despised it.'

My old friend Frank Lowe, of Bolton, visited Hermaness in 1925, when the watcher – Edwardson – had become known as 'Britain's loneliest man'. Edwardson had spent the spring and summer of thirty-seven years guarding the skuas, with no companion but his dog. Frank once saw that dog toppled by a diving bird. He was also entertained, early in the day, when a pair of bonxies dived repeatedly into a peat cutting where a raven had taken shelter. The raven periodically rose from the dyke, only to be chased back by the skuas. Eventually, the desperate bird made a dash for the coast.

Another visitor in the 1920s, T. A. Coward, trudged up Hermaness Hill, which he called 'Bonxie Hill' in a book, and met the faithful Edwardson. Coward spent most of his time watching the Arctic skua.

Whenever we were in what the scooties considered the danger zone, we knew about it. The cries became even more feline, with much emphasis on the second syllable – often a distinct *mee-ow*; and whilst one of the pair tumbled about the ground, just as if it had been badly wounded by gunshot, the other came at us with such an intensity of purpose that we winced as it skimmed over with a strange rip of wings. Sometimes half a dozen maimed birds were rolling in agony, with beaks wide open, wailing in great distress as they fanned an apparently helpless wing in their endeavour to regain their feet; but sympathy for these poor distressed fowls was wasted, for when we approached a sufferer it speedily rose and became aggressor. . . .

The Arctic skuas were on eggs, but some of the bonxies had young, which obediently crouched in the stunted ling and peat hags when the warning cries had been sounded. These infants were 'clad in wonderfully soft yellowish-brown down, with lead blue bills and feet. . . . They were not pleased when we handled them, and one presented us with its recent meal, which had had temporary quarters in at least three different throats and stomachs.'

The storm raged over Hermaness Hill. The hut in which I

sheltered creaked and strained. Some visitors in a similar plight to mine had drawn caricatures of seabirds on the wooden panelling within. Skua drawings were especially life-like, as well they might be, for live models were to be found close to the hut. I had watched a bonxie alight near its mate and assume that regal pose made familiar through photography. Neck and wings are extended, the wings being inclined backwards. Simultaneously the bird opens its ponderous beak and shouts into the storm.

The cloud mass thinned, then a few tatters of cloud swept by. I stepped out of the hut to find myself under a powder-blue sky and watched a skylark – surely the most northerly lark in Britain – rise like a feathered helicopter, brimming over with song. I trudged over the ridge and took the downhill path to the sea's edge, passing through a zone of deer-sedge and cotton-sedge. Tumbling cliffs confronted the Atlantic, which seethed around a line of stacks and skerries.

My eyes sought and found Outstack, or North Stack, Britain's most northerly piece of rock. The sea had smoothed and rounded the stack, and when one dedicated naturalist, Niall Rankin, managed to land many years ago, he found only one nest, that of a great black-backed gull, with a single nestling. Muckle Flugga, rising to 200 feet, gave the impression that it was leaning against tide and wind, and the lighthouse seemed to be the only true vertical. Wherever the rock is broken, a pair of gannets nest, their ivory bodies and the guano, splashed on the rock, giving to The Flugga the appearance of being hastily whitewashed.

Muckle Flugga! I cheered at the sight of this famous rock. When a navigational aid was put on its summit during the Crimean War, steps had to be hacked from the living rock; even so, the work was completed in less than a month. When it was decided to erect a permanent tower, a 'tin hut' was provided for the workmen. It is recorded that a rogue wave crashed on its roof.

Niall Rankin was in a relief boat in the days when the supplies for the lighthouse consisted of paraffin, coal, drinking-water and food. He counted 246 steps from the point of landing to the lighthouse. He related that a *green* sea had overtopped the rock, battered down the stone wall, smashed in a door at the foot of the lighthouse and swept away half the year's coal supply, the cobs tumbling down the rock's southern face.

The Flugga has its satellite stacks: Little Flugga, Tipta Skerry, Rumblings. The mainland cliffs look careworn – a jumble of faces, gullies, grassy slopes, the rocks painted with lichen and pockets of soil sporting the pinks of campion and sea-thrift.

Halfway down a cliff at Hermaness, a black-browed albatross squats on a ledge, as it has done for ten successive nesting seasons. This long-stay visitor from the southern oceans, which once excited bird-watchers at Bass Rock, in the Firth of Forth, goes through the ritual of nest-building, but no mate arrives. Nearby is a throng of gannets, part of a colony now totalling over 6,000 pairs that developed from the appearance of a few birds on Vesta Skerry towards the end of the 1914–18 war.

Puffins adorn the screes and grassy slopes, and far below are the guillemots, packed on the ledges in seemingly disordered array, but each bird mindful of its own little space and ready to defend it with a jab of the bill or a noisy growling, though constant action does mean that a bird may not stay in precisely the same spot. Razorbills abound on broken cliff. Shags build their compost-heaps on the large flat ledges near the sea. Kitti-wakes pitch their voices high, avoiding vocal competition with the other bird species and with the roaring sea. There are fulmars on patrol.

The bird spectacle of Hermaness extends to the sea and the rafts of off-duty or immature seabirds. Guillemots turn on the water, exposing their white underparts, preening with all the care of creatures that need immaculate, waterproofed feathers to survive at sea. Gannets arriving with fish are set upon by the bonxies that are flying sorties from Hermaness Hill.

To turn one's back on the smell and din, on the sight of thousands of gannets squatting on nests built on impossibly steep slopes, and guillemots looking like long rows of skittles, is to enjoy a sudden transformation. A few yards back from the cliff edge is the quieter world of the hill – quiet, that is, until a great skua decides to launch itself on one of those low-flying sweeps that brings it to within a foot or two of the intruder's left ear.

A skua that swept in from the sea had lowered its webbed undercarriage in anticipation, perhaps, of dealing me a blow. Or maybe those dangling legs helped it to maintain its equilibrium in the blustery air. The reason for its pugnacity was understandable.

I was standing near a nest, a shallow depression lined with bleached grasses, on which two eggs had been laid.

My journey to Hermaness thus began and ended with the buccaneering bonxies.

# 13

# Fetlar:
# White Owl and Phalarope

Near Baltasound, a pair of oystercatchers paraded their chicks. A few hours later, one of the adult birds was dead, a victim of fast traffic. The corpse of what had been a lively creature was squashed flat; the pied form, with half-opened wings, resembled a study in chalk made by a pavement artist. Curlews circled and yelped as their young flattened themselves against the sides of peaty hollows. A ringed plover chick moved on legs that seemed grotesquely large for such a dainty creature.

Near the ferry landing, an otter floated on a sun-flecked sea and was no more than ten feet from the shore. We stared at each other for what seemed like half an hour and was probably no more than ten seconds; then the otter dived, leaving a bubble-trail. So clear was the sea that I watched the creature's progress underwater; when the otter surfaced, some fifty yards away, it showed only its head, its back and the tip of its tail. Then I found myself looking at a miniature version of the Loch Ness monster. Shetland otters are largely marine, subsisting on fish and crabs, and if they do venture into a burn, it is usually to turn over the stones looking for eels.

I drove my car onto the ferry to visit 'the fat island', otherwise known as Fetlar and generally regarded as the 'garden' of Shetland. The ferry journey from Unst to Oddsta took twenty minutes, and once again I saw strings of seabirds moving up and down the sound between the islands. The appearance of skuas made me ponder on a topic that was on everyone's mind: the Falklands War. How like the Falklands these isles of Shetland looked, judging by the film I had seen on television. I scanned the low, bare ridges. I began to think of the skuas as marauding aircraft. A young man who stood beside me said: 'Have you heard the news?' And he told me that the conflict in the Falklands was at an end.

From Oddsta, I drove across moorland that was tonally dull under cloud. Then I broke the skyline, and much more of the island was revealed. Ahead of me lay a sweep of fertile croft land. Fetlar has variety: heath and grassland, clear lochs – some fresh, some salty – and considerable sea cliffs, with caves, natural arches and stacks. From an elderly native I heard of times that were – of families who lived in turf-huts at the peat-digging for days on end, who tended to lie up under cover during the hottest days and work in the coolness of the 'simmer dim', transporting the peat to the crofts in pony-borne panniers. On clear moonlit nights later in the year, families stayed up to set the arable crops into stooks.

On Fetlar, the curlew's nesting range overlaps that of its northern cousin, the whimbrel. A fifth of the British whimbrel population is spread over the moors of this tiny island. Those moors also hold stocks of golden plover, skua, dunlin and twite. Every lochan seems to have its resident pair of red-throated divers, and auks are massed at suitable stretches of the rocky coast. Arctic terns cloud the air. In the evening, Manx shear-waters are in flickering flight in the Wick (or Bay) of Tresta, and other birds sit on the water, waiting for that brief spell of summer darkness in which they can visit their nesting burrows on Lamb Hoga.

Storm-petrels dance in the air like bats, or churr and hiccough in their burrows as they effect the changeover in incubation duties, each bird sitting on an egg which looks no larger than a pea. Storm-petrels croak; they also smell! Sniff at some of the cracks and crannies on Lamb Hoga and you might detect an occupied burrow by its peculiar musty odour. The nesting season is comparatively late, beginning in June, extending until well into October, when the last of the young depart for the open sea.

The wind blows unchecked across ocean and hillock, and anything that is likely to grow higher than a lettuce is planted in the lee of a wall! Near the Kirk at Tresta, where a few trees snuggle behind a high wall, I noticed that the upper branches had been lacerated by the south-easterly gales. These, picking up speed over the North Sea, must at times have Fetlar shaking on its ancient foundations.

Fetlar achieved a special sort of fame in 1967. That summer, Bobby Tulloch was crossing a stretch of rocky ground known as

Stakkeberg with a party of bird-watchers when he excused him-self, walked a short distance from the party and located the nest of a pair of snowy owls, containing two white eggs. With im-mense self-control, he kept the discovery to himself. In due course, a sanctuary order was granted, and a 1,400-acre reserve came into being. The snowy owls bred annually until 1975, about twenty young birds being reared. Then the old male, which had been christened Snowy and had driven off potential rivals, vanished from the Fetlar scene. In 1975 only female owls were left, and that was the situation at the time of my visit.

The warden told me precisely where a snowy owl might be seen. Parking my car near the school, I watched another visitor depart at a jog-trot, unable to contain her excitement at seeing the big white owl in its moorland setting. The bird was reported to be sheltering beside a fencing post, within viewing range of the school. The owl-hunter rounded a corner of the building as I laced up my boots near the car. So eager was she to tick off 'snowy owl' on her list that I half-expected her to re-appear, still trotting, with the bird in her hands!

Snowy owls are typically birds of the high Arctic; though a number of pairs breed on the plateau of the Hardanger Vidda, in Norway, 300 miles from Shetland. Snowy owls can endure the Arctic winter because they are well lagged. Thick, polar-white feathers resist the bitter cold. They can also find food, descending on the Arctic hare and ptarmigan, which are two other creatures that moult into winter whiteness. Spring activates the snowy owl's main food source, which is the lemming, a tiny creature that has its numerical ups and downs, quite apart from the cull made by predators. The lemming population is cyclical. In a 'lemming year' the tundra teems with these squeaking little mammals. Assured of abundant food, the snowy owl increases its clutch size. As the lemming population crashes, some of the birds have no option but to drift southward. Shetland has had its vagrant 'snowies' down the years.

Such surplus birds may have formed the nucleus of the new breeding group, or the archipelago may have become more attractive following subtle changes in the climate, giving the owls more favourable breeding conditions, though they would have to look hard and long to find a lemming. The Shetland owls dine on woodmice, rabbits and birds and, being large, can surprise and subdue creatures as big as skuas.

With competition from the lady bird-watcher, my chance of seeing the owl appeared to be lost. To be fair, she did not rush about the moor. We heard a chorus of alarm calls. The snowy owl passed before us, pursued by common gull, redshank and lapwing. Our owl departed with dignity, resembling a white moth, though this being a female owl the plumage was barred with dark brown.

I was in prime whimbrel country, surrounded by heather and moss. This boreal curlew, the 'peerie whaup' to Shetlanders, winters by the sea in West Africa and may not return to its nesting grounds until May. The eggs are laid in early June. A hundred pairs of whimbrels, no more, may be nesting on the Scottish islands. Watchers on the Outer Hebrides in spring see whimbrels heading northwards – destination, almost certainly Iceland – and although the autumn migration is mainly along the coast, I have seen whimbrels loitering in the cowberry and crowberry country of the high Pennines, the berries offering rich nourishment in advance of a long migratory journey.

In early June, curlews were tending chicks, and whimbrels were sitting on clutches of pear-shaped eggs. As I walked on the mossy moor, a whimbrel circled with shallow wingbeats, contributing its high, clear and rippling notes to the moorland soundtrack. Standing on the moor, the bird blended with the duncoloured uplands, resembling a curlew in its sense of unease and in its plumage of vermiculated browns. When the whimbrel alighted on a knoll, breaking the skyline, I could see it was smaller, trimmer than the familiar curlew. The bill was noticeably shorter: maybe just a third of the length of a curlew's neb. The whimbrel flew, and the call – seven clear, rapid whistles – sent a shiver of pleasure down my spine.

The Fetlar bird I was most anxious to see is rare in the British context and is given special protection; it must not be disturbed where it nests. Some local birds have a favourite feeding loch named Funzie. And it was on the roadside, which here is almost part of the shoreline of the Loch of Funzie, that I parked my car. Funzie is small, yet not too small. Ringed by low hills, it stands apart from human habitations. The clear water laps against a mainly shingle beach. Four red-throated divers were in possession, the nearest diver being less than thirty yards away. I presumed that they were failed breeders. The birds preened and dozed. One of them rolled in the water, exposing its white underparts, which were given a delicate grooming. Another diver drifted, beak under a scapular, and ignored my car. So did the curlew, stalking in the shallows and then bathing, creaming the water with vigorous wingbeats. Elsewhere, calm water faithfully reflected the chestnut white and black of a dunlin's plumage. Arctic terns, using boulders as perches, surveyed other terns as they splashed in the shallows.

Along the edge of the loch, where the silvery water was broken by boulders in silhouette, a small bird was spinning on the water. It stopped briefly to pick up oddments of food with a bill that looked as fine as a needle. It had to be a phalarope! The bird was tiny indeed – no more than six inches in length. Yet this thin slip of a bird was constantly active, swimming buoyantly, moving incessantly, pecking at objects with the rapidity of the needle on a sewing-machine.

The red-necked phalarope, which looks so frail it might be blown over by a puff of wind, spends ten months of the year on the open sea, where in rough weather it is tossed about like a cork. It comes ashore for the brief nesting season and for a time may actually be out of the sight of salt water. The more brightly coloured female allows herself to be mated, lays a clutch of eggs and then departs. It is the male bird that, uncomplainingly, takes over the incubation of the eggs and rears the young. As soon as possible, these birds assemble on open water prior to migrating across the ocean to their winter quarters.

No more than fifty pairs of red-necked phalaropes nest in Britain, and a quarter of that population may be found on the island of Fetlar. The phalarope restlessly working the edge of the Loch of Funzie passed the car at a range of about fifteen feet, sporting its patch of orange-red plumage that extends like a horseshoe around the lower neck and reaches to the ear coverts. This diminutive seabird stood for a few moments, preened briskly, sprang into the air with a twittering call and became a dark dot against the immensity of the sky.

The *St Clair* sailed from Lerwick to Aberdeen at 6 p.m. It was a time for reflection. I thought of puffins, especially those I had seen at Noss. George Scott-Moncrieff, an author incapable of writing a dull phrase, said of them: 'They are grotesquely human and seem to fly like a man might fly, in vast doubt, trailing big boots through the air, apprehensively looking over his shoulder; and the bonxies and black-backs catch them in scores and empty out their little feathery hides and leave them all over the grass.'

I thought of skuas, and especially the Arctic skuas, so common on Unst and Fetlar and yet so rare in the national context. Only a thousand pairs nest in all Scotland. The isles of Shetland offer views of the little storm-petrels, which flutter like bats around the broch on Mousa and on slopes above lonely stretches of shore. Their status and distribution, for so long known imprecisely, have been revealed by tape-luring the birds: playing recorded calls and enmeshing those that respond. The birds are ringed, then released. In one year, on the island of Yell, the number of birds thus handled exceeded 3,000. With them were a few Leach's petrels.

Joining a Scotsman at the rail of the *St Clair*, I heard that he was redundant yet again. His five-year contract with a branch of the oil industry was ended. The camp at which he lived was being sold. 'They'll dig a big hole and bury what's left.' The oil industry, still comparatively new to the northern isles, is symbolised by the hilltop flame near Sullom Voe.

As the ferry left Lerwick, a tystie shifted its position, and bonxies followed us down the channel. Sumburgh Head slipped behind. Foula was seen lying under a dense mass of purple cloud, yet to the south lay a strip of clear sky which the declining sun had tinted a citrus yellow.

I chatted with an oil executive, off for a meeting, and I heard about the bonxie that joins herring-gulls at the dustbins of Sullom Voe. Together we watched the approach of Fair Isle, the island that has long been famous to ornithologists because of its observatory and has a familiar name to almost everyone because it features in the daily shipping forecasts. Lying midway between Sumburgh Head and North Ronaldsay, this speck of land in an often stormy sea is also world famous for its knitwear.

It is a living island. Crofters go about their ancient tasks, rarely looking at the clock, co-operating with rather than defying the condition of the land and the state of the climate. The Fair Islanders tend to keep calendar time; they adjust their routine to the slow progress of the seasons. The birds come and go, signifying the approach of spring and the departure of summer. The island's little boat, *Good Shepherd*, serves the island by sea, and Loganair maintains a regular schedule through the sky.

In early spring, the islanders watch the vacant lots on the cliffs fill up with auks, kittiwakes and fulmars. There are bonxies and Arctic skuas on the moors; they harass the sheep in their determination to keep the territories clear of intruders. The Fair Isle wren pitches its voice above the cries of the seabirds and the booming of the waves. Twites nest on both the moors and croftlands.

If the resident birds developed an interest in observing humans, they would note that the largest number was present in the autumn, migration time, when so often the gales exhaust or throw off their normal course those birds that are flying south for the winter. Fair Isle becomes a temporary haven for the migrant birds, and a place of ecstacy for those who travel here to watch them.

Before the 1914–18 war, Eagle Clarke was on Fair Isle studying the bird traffic, and his pioneer surveys encouraged others to take an interest in this branch of ornithology. George Waterston bought Fair Isle after the 1939–45 war, and an observatory was opened. Kenneth Williamson became its first warden. Since 1954, Fair Isle has been owned by the National Trust for Scotland – and the list of birds recorded here is well over 300 species.

In a lingering twilight, the *St Clair* passed near Sheep Rock, a block of sandstone over 400 feet high which is joined to the mainland by a sliver of crumbling rock. Later, I saw a new windvane, installed for the generation of electricity and virtually guaranteed enough wind to operate it.

I was standing on deck at 10.30 p.m. when the sun found the clear strip of sky in the west. Gold light tipped the waves. Next morning, I awoke to a summer murk, through which I could just make out the Bullers of Buchan. The cliffs were splashed by the droppings of countless seabirds.

An eider at its nest, which is lagged with down the bird has plucked from its breast; this down is drawn over the eggs when the duck leaves for a short spell. Young eider have a hazardous journey to the sea, running the gauntlet of predatory gulls

The crowded world of the guillemot. There are heavy concentrations of birds on suitable cliffs and stacks, such as St Abbs, on the south-east coast of Scotland. Pear-shaped eggs are laid on the bare rock

Newly hatched cormorants. They are naked at first, and it is vital that they should be covered by a parent bird, whatever the weather

A nestling cormorant, pictured at a colony in the Firth of Forth. The quills encasing the flight feathers are just visible

A typical nest of a pair of oystercatchers on the shore, though this species is also found well inland, beside rivers and even on peat workings

The adult oystercatcher shown here was an inland bird. Notice its alert stance, handsome pied plumage and pick-axe bill

Razorbills in flight. These birds were photographed at the Mull of Galloway as they zoomed in from the sea. The narrow wings, so effective as paddles underwater, must be beaten furiously to keep the bird in the air. The birds pictured above were close to stalling as they neared their nesting sites

A low-slung autumn sun accentuates the graceful lines of a whooper swan on a merse just north of the Solway. Most of our whoopers come from Iceland, but ringing has established that a few originate in northern Russia

A family party of whooper swans on the merse at East Park, Caerlaverock. The gander is on the left

A fly-past of Spitzbergen barnacle geese at Caerlaverock. Seen distantly are the cooling towers at a power station near Annan

The barnacle goose, which has a migratory flight of almost 2,000 miles from its breeding grounds within the Arctic Circle

A salmon net is hung up to dry on the Solway shore

Ailsa Craig, in the Firth of Clyde. The shape has been compared to an upturned pudding basin. Thousands of Irish people passed it on their way to Glasgow, and it became known as Paddy's Milestone

# 14

# Black Isle:
# In Darkest Ross-shire

Cromarty is really a winter firth. The flutter of ten thousand wings is heard in the frosty stillness. A wigeon gives its cheery whistle, *whee-ou*. Grey geese chatter among themselves as they decorate the sky with chevrons, and a series of bugle calls announces the arrival of a family party of whooper swans.

Beside the shallow bays are assemblies of dunlin, knot, redshank, bar-tailed godwit and golden plover, all in their pale winter garb. There are dark carpets of oystercatchers and lapwings. A curlew briefly trills, as though rehearsing for the springtime aria; then, alert and suspicious, this long-nebbed bird stops many another wader in its tracks with a penetrating alarm call, *kour-lee*.

A flow tide scours the Sutors of Cromarty and then spreads itself along the fifteen miles of the firth. When a north-east wind is behind the tide, the water surges like a sea in captivity. Promontories break the backs of the waves; wildfowl mass in sheltered waters. Next day, conditions are good enough for the ducks, and the waders to admire their reflections in the water. When alarmed, teal spring from the water and put on a display of high-speed flying that would make a human pilot envious. Shelduck waddle on the low-tide mud. And all the time the wigeon call. There are thousands of wigeon. Cromarty Firth is the fourth most important wintering ground for wildfowl in Britain.

I knew Cromarty nearly forty years ago. In those days, a wood-and-concrete warship, HMS *Fieldfare*, stood on the Cromarty shore near Evanton. Noticing the bird-active sky, I requested (not just asked for!) the loan of some Service binoculars so that I could watch the birds. The First Lieutenant who granted that request told me of the flock of golden plover he had seen on the main runway. Arctic terns had nested on a shingle ridge. One winter afternoon, clasping my powerful binoculars, I parted frosted vegetation near the shore and came face to face with another senior officer. Rank was forgotten as we jointly watched the birds, also the seals basking on the sandbars.

I saw Cromarty from the summit of Fyrish – a summit I shared with white hares and Sir Hector Munro's curious embellishment, said to resemble the gate of Negapatam in India. I also saw the Black Isle. It was not black, neither was it an island. The *First Statistical Account of Scotland* (1791–9) accounted for the name by mentioning an abundance of black peat. Local people insisted that it is 'black' because in winter, when Fyrish and Ben Wyvis are whitened by snow, none lingers on the Black Isle, which is bounded by firths, lies in a salty air and looks distinctly dark in relation to the gleaming hills to the west. A third explanation is that some ancient scribe mistranslated the name. The Gaelic Eilean Dubhthaich – or the isle of St Duthac, patron saint of Tain – became Eilean Dubh, which means 'Black Isle'.

The peninsula is firmly tethered to the mainland, not only by a sliver of land but by two modern bridges. One crosses the Kessock narrows near Inverness, and the other spans Cromarty Firth. Those bridges have reduced the journey from Inverness to the North by some twelve miles and, more importantly, if you are a businessman, have provided better access to the new industrial plants on the northern shore of Cromarty.

Forty years ago, the Sutors – those sentinels at the mouth of the firth – were a never-ending source of fascination to me. I took the ferry and went to the South Sutor to watch fulmars. The ferryman told me of the King's Causeway that followed the ridge on the Black Isle – a pilgrim's route, ending at Tain, where homage could be paid to St Duthac. We returned, the ferryman and I, amid clouds of birds. At a time when the Sunderland flying-boat was the largest aircraft that many of us had seen, I remember comparing its general appearance with the mute swans we disturbed. A swan would lumber into flight, working its wings hard, pattering on the water with its large webbed feet, then lifting into the air to become a graceful flying object. The flying-boats needed plenty of sea room.

Cromarty's most famous son, Hugh Miller – stonemason, geologist, author – considered that the sutors were 'one of a chain belonging to the great Ben Nevis line of elevation . . . a huge primary mass, upheaved of old from the abyss, and composed chiefly of granitic gneiss and a red splintery hornstone'. There was a much more fantastic explanation: that two giant cobblers used the bastions of Cromarty Firth as their benches. Souter was a local name for cobbler; the passage of time shortened it to 'sutor'.

The Black Isle is almost a kingdom unto itself. This slab of Old Red Sandstone lies between the firths which are among the few indentations in the north-east coastline; firths with extensive mudflats and expanses of eelgrass to nourish the wintering ducks and waders. Beauly Firth offers sanctuary and food for divers, greylags and red-breasted mergansers. In summer it welcomes Canada geese on a moult-migration from the Harrogate district of Yorkshire.

I crossed to the Black Isle using the new Cromarty Bridge, with its 110 piers. I spent a day on an 'island' which impresses me with its light and colour. The sea shimmers. Hedge-bordered fields have woodland settings. As I strode along the beach from Rose-markie, to see the finest cliffs, I noticed a geological hotchpotch. Boulders protruding from the sand were in a variety of pastel shades: one red, one yellow, yet another grey, and one so streaked with red that it resembled a chunk of raw flesh.

Old writers mentioned 'black woods', which were coniferous, dominated by the Scots pine. Dark, drool pines occupy the central ridge of the Black Isle, where once the local people grazed their cattle and collected peat. The Isle is noted for its Scots pines, which are tended by the Forestry Commission. While gathering cones for propagation, a rifleman on the ground fires up at them. Shrewdly, he has donned a helmet! A crashing sound among the secondary growth may be from a forester in difficulty but is more likely to be a departing capercaillie, the largest grouse in the world, which when flying has a reckless disregard for minor obstructions. A few crested tits flutter around the crowns of the trees; look for them in this setting and you will surely have neckache. At nesting time, the wee birdies use holes in rotting trees as the nurseries for their eggs.

Strange tales are told of the Black Isle, which was noted for witchcraft. The pagan past blends with modern times on Undie Sunday, the unofficial name for a custom of attaching multi-strips of cloth to the trees near an ancient wishing-well. I saw the annual display on the day of my visit. I took the road from Muir of Ord through Tore and Munlochy and on to the seaside at Avoch, where the local people are said to be descended from survivors of the wreck of a Spanish galleon.

Several times I drew the car to a halt near a post on which a buzzard stood like a feathered totem. Buzzards circled and mewed over the bountiful woodland. Shelduck fussed over young birds that were patterned like old-fashioned humbugs. The adults were splendidly marked, the white of the plumage being banded by dark green, chestnut and black. A female – she lacked the knob at the base of the bill – scythed the freshly exposed mud, seeking molluscs and crustaceans.

Gannets wheeled and glided over herring-rich waters. Cromarty throve with the old 'herring-drove', which resulted in the exportation of thousands of barrels of prime fish. The story of one exceptional drove was related by Miller, and it happened 'shortly after the Union' (of 1707). With whales and porpoises at their tails, herrings were stranded in a bay a few hundred yards to the east of the town. That beach was said to have been covered to a depth of several feet, 'and salt and casks failed the packers when only an inconsiderable part of the shoal was cured. The residue was carried away for manure by the neighbouring farmers, and so great was the quantity used in this way, and the stench they caused so offensive, that it was feared disease would have ensued.'

The herring shoals were fickle and just as likely to desert. The herrings forsook Cromarty Firth, and religious folk pronounced it a judgement because the packers continued to work through Saturday into Sunday. According to superstition, harvest ended when two men fought, leaning over the gunwales of their respective boats. Blood had been spilt in the sea! Herrings, the superstitious continued, have a strong antipathy to human blood, especially when shed in a quarrel.

Sandwich and Arctic terns swept the sea or hovered above likely sources of food. The creaky sounds made by the terns gave the impression that their slender wings were moving on rusty hinges.

Rain swept the Black Isle. Colour drained from Rosemarkie, which is normally a bright place, renowned for its displays of roses. The great black-backed gulls on the stacks called peevishly, as well they might in the conditions. Cormorants, clad in undertaker black, left the rocks with a flurry of leathery wings. Rock doves zoomed from small caves, and jackdaws appeared from behind curtains of ivy that draped themselves from cliff faces.

I travelled from the Black Isle to the Black Wood – to Glen Affric, with its bountiful forest of Scots pine, birch and juniper, plus a rich and varied ground flora. For a time I exchanged the boom of the sea, the hiss of water against shingle and the seabird chorus for an area of quiet dignity, such as you might experience in an ancient, multi-pillared cathedral. In a commercial forest, lines of trees are drawn up like troops on parade. Wordsworth had the new larch plantations of the Lake District in mind when he wrote about 'vegetable manufactory'. Glen Affric offered the flavour of Old Caledonia, a forest that had regenerated naturally. Wood ants had heaped up pine needles and nested within the heap. Crossbills tore at cones and sent the inedible parts dribbling to the ground. The twitter of the crested tit would not have stood a chance of being heard by the sea. In the still depths of the 'black wood', the churring of a blue tit had the effect of a pneumatic drill!

Other human visitors scoured the pebbly banks of the river near Dog Fall, looking for garnets, which were like inflamed boils on some of the water-worn stones. The hydro-electricity board had plugged the glen to provide a head of water, which appealed to a red-throated diver, a bird that later uttered its eerie wail. The moorland beyond Affric Lodge had scarcely a bird upon it, but there was compensation in the beauty of the isolated pines, each tree a character, of individualistic appearance and looking very old. The sun's rays were absorbed by a bottle-green foliage, and where bark had peeled from the upper parts of the trees, that selfsame sun produced an orangy glow with the coming of evening. A hooded crow harassed a raven, which turned and offered the full extent of its dark wings to the view of the low-slung sun, so that they were shot with silver.

Of the glens near Inverness, a special favourite is Strathconan, though here again a hydro-electricity undertaking has robbed the river of some of its spirit. I recalled what the poet Norman Nicholson had written about Haweswater, in the Lake District. When the dale was dammed, the intermediate land between the old water level and the hills had vanished from sight. Henceforth, a visitor saw great hills standing up to their waists in cold water! Within half an hour I viewed a trilogy of noble birds: buzzard, peregrine falcon and golden eagle. My first eagle of the day, its size judged in relation to the buzzard, had found a thermal and lazily trimmed its feathers to the updraught, to be carried high with no further physical effort. A peregrine falcon stirred it from its reverie by stooping on it. Plainly, the eagle and the peregrine were nesting in the same area.

Where a peat-brown river surged over grey boulders, oyster-catchers shouted abuse from the riverbank. Common gulls became excited around an island composed of shingle. I went in search of nests. There were two, one nest empty and the other containing three eggs – until the next freshet.

I detected an air of sadness in the upper part of the valley. Before the Clearances, this strath was well populated, and something of the old grandeur remains at a Telford church. Elsewhere, one was aware of the glory that had departed. The strath narrowed. About forty red stags grazed a large field in daylight. One or two 'old boys' had cast their antlers and were now beginning the unsightly process of losing the winter coat.

I lay on my back near the infant watercourse, scanning the weather-seamed cliff beyond. I lay because the hills were tall, leaping directly from the narrow glen. It was a pair of ravens that directed my attention to a tattered skyline of frost-cracked rocks. When a raven or a crow is calling, there is usually something interesting to be seen. Those ravens dived at a golden eagle, which – doubtless knowing them of old – calmly took the necessary evasive action. When a raven seemed hell-bent on colliding with the eagle, the latter avoided disaster by simply drawing in a wing, the raven passing so closely that it must have rocked the idling eagle. This large bird drifted along the ridge, and the hoarse voices of the ravens were stilled.

Raven Rock, near Strathpeffer, was approached along a puddly path, each puddle a mass of tadpoles. They seethed as my shadow fell across them. A stoat that bounded nearby was still partly in its winter white. Siskin and redpoll decked the waterside alders and rummaged among the tree buds for grubs. The Rock dominates a deep cutting made when the railway link with Kyle was established. As I arrived, the 11.10 a.m. train passed with a clatter and plume of smoke from the diesel's exhaust. The calls of ravens echoed in the confined space of a partly man-made gorge. The raven nest was the usual bundle of large twigs.

Later, not far from Strathpeffer, I watch a pair of buzzards – and patted a stone eagle. The buzzards nested in the upper fork of a Scots pine, one of a cluster between a hillside ragged with gorse and a lochan rowdy with ducks. The incubating bird flew as I passed; I stopped for a few moments and heard the first of a series of ringing calls. A testy 'whoodie' came to investigate the hubbub and to harry the buzzard, which took evasive action with a weary acceptance that it had a crow in its territory.

Eagle Rock, at the edge of town, is Pictish in origin. Local people related an old tale that if the Rock fell over, Strathpeffer would be flooded. The Rock had fallen – twice. Now the townsfolk rest comfortably in their beds. They set the old carved stone in a bed of concrete!

# 15

# The East Coast:
# A Profusion of Kittiwakes

Dunnet Head, the Bullers of Buchan, Fowlsheugh, Dunbar, St Abbs Head – these formidable cliffscapes, widely separated, present a common front to the North Sea, and they have in common a conspicuous seabird: the kittiwake. Half a million pairs of kittiwakes nest in Britain and Ireland, and the majority are in colonies on the eastern seaboard, from the northern tip of Shetland to Flamborough Head. The kittiwake's gentle appearance belies its robust nature. It nests on cliffs, and it winters far from land. Even John Colquhoun, the Victorian sportsman, acknowledged its beauty – before he slew a pair at one discharge of his gun. The 'beautiful little gulls . . . toppled almost into the boat'.

The carnage is over. Women no longer rush to wear kittiwake feathers in their hats, as they did in Victorian days. The eggs are no longer gathered as food. One collector was named Adams. Last century, he rented the Bass Rock, collecting as many 'gull and kittiwake eggs' as he could. It was a time when the eggs of auks were taken to be blown and the shells were prized for their eccentric patterning. One man described guillemot eggs as 'rank-tasted'.

Dip your toe in the North Sea, even in summer, and you will wince at the coldness, yet these are 'warm' waters to the kittiwake tribe, which here is at the southern end of a vast breeding range. Cold water, ceaselessly stirred so that the nutrient salts are active, allowing the sunlight to work its annual miracle of making the sea bloom, provides rich feeding for kittiwakes. At Dunnet Head, the most northerly point on the British mainland, with a mere six- or seven-mile gap between here and the most southerly island of Orkney, the cliffs rang with kittiwake calls. A bird which tends to be silent when at sea can be extremely noisy on land, especially when there is an excited reunion between birds of a pair.

The kittiwake is a bird of wild water. A change of tide in the Pentland Firth produces a turmoil of surging, swirling, crashing waves. I journeyed southwards to where kittiwakes decked the cliffs at the Bullers of Buchan, south of Peterhead. The rousing cries – *kitti-wa-a-k, kitti-wa-a-k* – reverberated in a splendid echo chamber. I refer to a 'cauldron' with deep sides, the sea entering it through a natural arch. Johnson and Boswell were here in 1773. Boswell noticed that the arch was too narrow for oars to be used, and so 'the method taken is to row very hard when you come near it, and give the boat such rapidity of motion that she glides in.' The good doctor gambolled on the edge of this natural amphitheatre. Johnson was also taken into the Buller by boat.

Kittiwakes doubtless made the area ring with noise in 1814, when Walter Scott was rowed into the confined area, between walls of dark rock. He saw nothing above 'but the blue sky'. To Scott, those local people who watched his party from the brink were like 'sylphs looking down on gnomes'.

Massed kittiwakes decked the cliff at Fowlsheugh, just south of Stonehaven. This stretch of coast lies near one of the busiest roads in Scotland, the one leading to and from Aberdeen. The cliff-nesting gulls, plus the teeming auks, nest on a mile-long cliff that has a maximum height of 200 feet. Guillemots pack the ledges. Razorbills use holes left when small boulders were displaced, and puffins are also in evidence. Shags disappear mysteriously into sea-edge caves. This coastline is unstable; one should move with care. The safest approach is from Crawton, at the southern end. Those who walk from Dunottar Castle must watch their step, but their reward is the sight of eiders in the bays, herring-gulls on the shore and – on and around Trelung Ness, the major cliff – a blizzard of wheeling kittiwakes.

Dunbar, in East Lothian, occupies a rocky headland. The entrance channel to the latest of several harbours was blasted from sandstone with a disregard of what remained of the ancient castle. Victorian engineers ruined the ruins! Boats enter harbour to a shrill welcome from the kittiwakes, the sound reverberating in the confined space. Some kittiwakes nesting on rock ledges below the castle are close to a busy harbour and yet out of sight of the sea. These kittiwakes are also within stroking distance of the visitors! To a prospecting kittiwake, a ledge is a ledge, and at Dunbar man unwittingly provided sites for these ocean birds when he constructed large warehouses near the harbour. The window-ledges have made first-rate nesting ledges for a number of enterprising pairs.

A chorus of kittiwakes echoed and re-echoed against the cliffs all the way from St Abbs Head to Fast Castle, a fortress perched on a pinnacle and referred to, as Wolf's Crag, by Walter Scott in his *Bride of Lammermoor*. The sweeping Lammermuir Hills end abruptly at St Abbs in a range of reddish cliffs. St Cuthbert, who was born on the Lammermuirs, visited St Ebba's small religious house at nearby Coldingham, and – this being Cuthbert – the act of faith had to be accompanied by deprivation. He spent the greater part of one night in prayer and vigil while standing up to his neck in the sea!

St Abbs Head, owned by the National Trust for Scotland and managed jointly with the Scottish Wildlife Trust, is like a stone fist clenched against the fury of the North Sea. There is a lighthouse on the rim, 275 feet above the sea. A footpath from the village leads to a bird cliff that is striated horizontally by ledges and the white droppings from nesting seabirds. Viewed on a misty day, it resembles a chunk of primitive sculpture. Here the kittiwake colonies form apartment blocks in unpromisingly steep places.

At any of the big east-coast nesting stations, the kittiwakes are easy to watch. They do not mind being peered at from a range of a few yards. This gentle-looking gull has a subdued colouring. To Edward A. Armstrong they were 'birds painted in watercolour'. There is black in the scheme: eyes black as ebony, wings tipped with black. Yet the beak is a delicate lime-yellow. When the mandibles are open, an orange gape is revealed. In general shape, size and markings, the kittiwake resembles the common gull, which nests on our Scottish islets and moorlands. Compared with a big gull, the kittiwake seems dainty, light and buoyant, resting on the air like thistledown.

In winter, big gulls squabble at the urban rubbish tips. Herring-gulls descend to collect pieces of bread tossed away on seaside promenades. Black-headed gulls risk decapitation by plough-shares as they dart into new-cut furrows behind the busy plough. The kittiwake is, meanwhile, far out at sea. When the bird is not at its breeding quarters, it ranges the North Atlantic, dining on plankton and small fish.

Within a few months of taking its first flight, the 'tarrock' – a name given to the young kittiwake – may have crossed the Atlantic, gliding off the coast of Newfoundland or wheeling over the Grand Banks. In the following summer, it may make a northward journey to the rich waters off the west coast of Greenland. Three years are spent maturing, in becoming wise to the ways of the sea, and yet a knowledge of the natal area is retained through the bird's exile. In due course, it returns to the area where it was hatched, steering as positively as the home-running salmon looking for the river in which it was hatched.

The kittiwake is a gull that adapted to life on the cliff face. Its nesting territory may be little more than the nest itself, set precariously on a ledge or knob abutting sheer rock. Here at least it is safe from land-based predators, and the herring-gull – ever on the scrounge for eggs or young birds, of its own or other species – would find it difficult to settle on a kittiwake nest long enough to cause damage to the family. It needs a special technique to touch down safely within an inch or two of a rock wall. Esther Sager, a notable watcher of kittiwakes on the Farne Islands, found that these birds paid scant attention to predators. The alarm call of the kittiwake is not often heard.

From a perch on a cliff top, ten yards from the nearest kittiwake nest, I marvelled again at the bird's ready acceptance of human company at close range. Yet the 'gentle' kittiwake can be quarrelsome. When the cliff's vacant lots are being filled in spring, every bird wishes to be at the central part of the colony, and there are fights for possession of prime sites. This species is markedly gregarious and away from the nest it likes company, such as when plunge-diving for food, washing in some freshwater loch or collecting grass from the cliff-top for the nest. I watched a score of birds tugging and tussling on quite a small tract of cliff-top, which by evening was little more than bare earth.

The pairs form on the ledges. It is a slow process. Strangers gradually become friends. Mutual distrust is supplanted – not without bickering – by mutual toleration. The birds call as they display. They perch, face to face, waving their heads, bowing with a grave dignity. The nests are deep pouches, and some actually overhang the sea. The grass collected at the clifftop has been worked in with seaweed and mud to create a nest that is so unlike the nests of other gulls. The number of eggs laid in a kittiwake nest, usually two as compared with the three or four produced by a large gull, is related to the effort needed to collect food for the young.

Niko Tinbergen and Esther Sager drew special attention to the feeding process – the transference of food from male to female, or from adult bird to young. Other gulls are inclined to drop food on the ground for collection by the young. With the kittiwakes, on their tight little nests high above the raging sea, the recipient pecks into the throat of the bird with the food. There is no wastage. The constricted nesting site inhibits movement. A young kittiwake stays put; it is inches from possible disaster. I watched a tarrock painstakingly turn to defecate into space. Towards the end of the season, nests that have been trampled by the young birds seem little more than platforms. It is not unknown for a kittiwake nest to collapse, spilling its contents, and winter gales demolish many another nest.

A pair of kittiwakes attend to their two eggs for about twenty-five days. During the fledgling period of six or seven weeks, a shift system with food is operated. With the sea crashing against rocks a hundred feet or so below the nest, a tarrock that makes an involuntary flight or does not judge the conditions aright has no chance of returning for a second try.

In mid-August, when the nesting bustle is over, and the auks have departed, the few remaining kittiwakes occupy themselves in various ways or simply doze on what remains of the nests. I watched two tarrocks preen, as they must if the plumage is to be kept clean and waterproof. Other youngsters took trial flights. One alighted on the remains of an old nest, shuffled its wings and then turned to defecate over the edge. Habits acquired in infancy are difficult to break. The young were easily identified, for dark grey feathers formed the shape of a W across their wings, and their necks were banded with black.

The kittiwake has come into its own. The exploitation of seabirds in the nineteenth century checked the population. Birds were sought as food or shot for 'sport' or captured so that their fine feathers could be used for ladies' headgear. In the period from 1880 to 1890, the first wave of legislation protected the seabirds, and the result was a spectacular spread of gannet, fulmar and kittiwake. Long-established kittiwake colonies became more densely packed. New nesting areas were prospected. Lower cliffs came into use, and few pairs have tried nesting on open ground, as did their ancestors before they adapted themselves to life on cliff faces.

# 16

# Bass Rock:
# A Temple for Gannets

A rogue wave collided with the harbour wall at North Berwick and dissipated its energy in a geyser-like column of white water. Yet the sun presided over a cloudless sky, and there was little wind. Stirred by recent storms, bubbling over from some remote oceanic cauldron, the sea exploded against rocks and seethed on the beaches. Eiders, undeterred by the wild conditions, paddled over walls of green water – straddling the foamy crests before plunging into the ink-blue troughs beyond – or they swam through the waves. One duck moved only when a curling wave cast a shadow over it!

The boisterous sea delayed my visit to the Bass Rock, a temple of the North Atlantic gannet, the scientific name of which, *Sula Bassana*, incorporates that of the famous Rock, which is a volcanic plug in the outer reaches of the Firth of Forth. North Berwick, renowned as the embarkation point, is a neat little town, with its own conical hill, known as The Law, the Bass's land-locked cousin, being of similar age and composition.

The Forth, really a vast tidal inlet, is spattered with islands. The names of some of them are incorporated in a little poem:

> *Inchgarvrie, Mickery, Colm, Inchkeith,*
> *Cramond, Fidra, Lamb, Craigleith:*
> *Then round the Bass to the Isle of May*
> *And past the Carr to St Andrew's Bay.*

Add to this merry collection the tiny island of Inchmickery, where roseate terns breed between the ugly remnants of wartime occupation by man. At the other end of the scale is the 143-acre Isle of May, accessible by boat from Anstruther and from Pitten-weem in Fife. The Isle of May is used by nesting seabirds, though its chief fame is as an observatory, established in 1934. In an area

where bird-watchers have been inclined to break out into verse, a
frustrated visitor wrote in the logbook:

> *There was an old man on the May*
> *Who knelt on the North Ness to pray.*
> *'Oh, Lord, I have sinned –*
> *But why need the wind*
> *Blow westerly, day after day?'*

What is an ill wind to ordinary mortals brings to the Isle of May
one of its celebrated 'falls' of uncommon birds. You can number
among them bluethroat, barred warbler and Lapland bunting.
Sea-watchers observe a grand fly-past of skuas and shearwaters,
on their autumn manœuvres. Near large, shallow bays are more
birds in passage: long-tailed duck, diver, skua, shearwater, tern
and, maybe, a little gull. The wintering wildfowl include scoter,
golden-eye, wigeon and greylag.

The islands give a Hebridean flavour to the Firth of Forth. They
rise, round-shouldered, from expanses of uneasy water. Perhaps
the local custom of enthusing in verse began with the Anglo-
Saxon nature poets who sang about the raging sea, about the cries
of gannet and curlew, about the mewing gull, the ice-feathered
tern and the screeching sea eagle.

See the Bass Rock from Dunbar, to the south, and it is just a
grey smudge on the horizon. Geologically, this is what was left
when molten lava set in the neck of a volcano, and the surrounding material was washed away. From Tantallon Castle – little
more than a mile from the Bass – fine detail is possible. This plug
of basalt looks out of context, like a gigantic piece of stage scenery
tethered in the Forth. It is owned by the National Trust for
Scotland. The white form of the lighthouse and some ancient
fortifications are clear to see from Tantallon. The Rock gleams,
white as chalk. It is not composed of chalk, of course, but is a dark
rock stained white by the gannets.

On my visit, the Bass stood in a boiling sea, three miles from
where I lodged. If I awoke during the brief night, the loom of the
Bass lighthouse bathed the ceiling. Awakened at dawn by the
Friendly Neighbourhood Herring Gull sounding reveille from a
chimney-pot, I sat up in bed to scan the sea – and the Rock. When
the sun set like a fireball, the Bass was bathed in pink light. A

visitor who heard me mention Bass thought I was talking about the brewery; the name actually means 'a cone-shaped rock'.

The museum at North Berwick held cases of stuffed gannets and other seabirds. The Northumbrian nature poet had revered the birds; later generations tended to think of them in commercial terms. The twelfth-century laird of Bass, who cherished his gannets, was in dispute with the nuns of North Berwick with regard to the barrels of gannet fat he should have made available as tithes. Young gannets were eaten, skinned and gutted, served 'a little before dinner'. From the flayed skin and intestines came an oil that alleviated gout and also – for good measure – diseases of the haunches and groins. (The oil found favour in the lubrication of axles of carts and machinery in local mills.)

John Colquhoun's *The Moor and the Loch*, a Victorian's chronicle of a sporting life, includes notes on Bass Rock and its gannets. The author had shot seafowl on the Clet of Caithness; he had stalked seals under the cliffs of Morayshire, 'but there is a grandeur about this solitary giant of the deep which is different from any of the wildest scenes I had gazed upon before.' As the boatman pulled slowly under a beetling cliff, which was studded from top to bottom with gannets, Colquhoun was paralysed rather than impressed with the 'stupendous scene'.

The wild waves that overawed me at North Berwick spent themselves. An uneasy swell moderated with every passing hour. Since my last visit, the boatman had invested in a larger craft. On a previous excursion, a sea-fret clung to the coast, and the foghorn's blasts were like notes from a Wagnerian opera. The Bass Rock was drained of colour. The sea remained too choppy for a landing, however brief. I recall that, as we sailed in the lee of Bass, two gannets, locked together, beak to beak, tumbled from the heights and maintained their grip even when they reached the water. The boatman later tossed some fragments of fish which he had intended to use as fishing-bait, from the boat, and gannets dived for them, hitting the water with such force that I was soaked by wind-blown spray.

The Bass Rock, a 350-foot stub of igneous rock, a mile in circumference, was in view from the moment the boat left North Berwick. Gannets were homing on the rock: they are goose-sized birds, also known as solan geese, from the Norse *sula*. White, cigar-shaped bodies and black-tipped wings were framed by the blues of sky and sea. The homing instinct is well developed in young gannets, and though they may be absent from northern waters for a year or two, they contrive to return to the Bass after a sojourn in the Mediterranean. The mature birds do not wander far and begin to return early in the year – months before the eggs are laid. In the meantime, there are courtship rites, some territorial bickering, the assembly of vegetation for the nest. Birds arrive with streamers of vegetation draped from their beaks, and an inattentive pair runs the risk of having the material, so painstakingly gathered, filched by the neighbours.

The boat cruised near the Bass, under the gaze of gannets sitting on their nest-drums, croaking to each other. A sitting bird greeted a returning mate with ecstatic calling and much bill-rubbing. Immature birds, not yet whiter-than-white, crowded the less important ledges. A herring-gull spiked a gannet egg and gobbled down the contents.

A gannet in the hand is worth two on the Rock. The boatman steered an unexpected course; he let the boat's engine idle and reached over the gunwale to gather up a gannet that had become entangled in plastic fishing-net. Such netting may provide a decorative touch to a gannet's nest, but it can also snare both adults and young birds, so that wasted bodies dangle from the ledges. It was clearly not the first time this boatman had rescued a gannet in distress. In minutes, he had the bird free. I watched him work with the gannet's mandibles held open to enable the bird to breath normally, for the nostrils are located within the beak. It was a lance-like beak, blueish in tone, with dark lines extending towards the black facial skin that encircled the ice-blue eyes, set in a straw-yellow head. Long after I had forgotten the fine points of the gannet, I was to remember the bird's penetrating stare!

On being released, the gannet fluttered for a few yards, then pitched on the sea, paddling away haughtily, riding high in the water, its long, pointed tail inclined upwards. Bryan Nelson, in his monograph of the gannet – compiled largely from observations and on Bass Rock over a long period – quotes comments made by Clyde fishermen to Angus Martin. The gannet, 'that imperial fish-hunter', had led many fishermen to good catches of fish. 'His presence was always investigated if his behaviour suggested that he might be working on herring.' Donald McIntosh told Martin that 'when ye see them hingin' yon wey, cockin'

their nebs, that's when the herrin' wir right thick.' A fisherman
who came across a full-bellied gannet on the surface would prod
it with an oar. The bird regurgitated the content of its stomach to
lighten itself and take off. The fisherman was able to discover the
nature of the bird's prey. He hoped it was herring!

We circumnavigated the Rock. The mouth of a cave gave the
appearance that the island was yawning. I came under the stare
of puffins: 'Tammie Norrie o' the Bass; Canna kiss a young lass.'
Everyone is captivated by puffins, and the booklet about Bass
Rock compared the birds with 'old men in bright orange carpet
slippers'!

It was time for a landing. The boat was brought to a range of
stone steps leading to where a helicopter pad had been made,
close to the old fortifications. The stubby lighthouse occupies a
higher ledge on a Rock where there is precious little level ground.
The path I followed lay between groves of tree mallow (*Lavatera
arborea*), the woody stems of which rose for over six feet and held
an array of rose-coloured flowers. Tree mallow swamped the
ruins of St Baldred's little chapel, though it is doubtful if the saint
himself had anything more elaborate than a cell. He lived long
before the chapel was built. Did he sleep on a mattress made of
gannet feathers? Where did he drink? The well I saw near the
chapel held a rich algal bloom.

The foetid odour of seabird droppings swirled over the cliff.
Gannets, part of a colony of 7,500 pairs, plus the immature birds,
lay about the head of a rock and ignored me. Bryan Nelson, in his
monograph, mentions the gannet's ritualised display by which
the social order is maintained. Some savage and punishing fights
take place at the nest site, which is defended by threat and
jabbing. The nest itself is highly functional in safeguarding the
egg and chick. Dr Nelson discovered a most useful way of
distinguishing a male gannet from a female. The veins on the
male's webbed feet are green, those of the female being turquoise.

The gannetry had spread from the edge of Bass Rock to the
peaty pate of the island. The birds were most densely packed, of
course, away from the sheer cliffs; in the more level areas the
arrangement was so neat – each sitting bird being just outside the
pecking range of its neighbours – that it might have been arranged
with the help of a computer. There was much coming and going

of birds. The arrival of a gannet was impressive. In the final stage before touch-down, the body was close to vertical, the wings inclined and the tips extended forward, arresting the forward speed, and the feet acted like the flaps of an aircraft. Bowing and bill-scissoring occupied the attention of re-united pairs. Along the edge of the colony, where the pairs were less well established, a high level of excitement was detected, and there was much robbery of nesting material.

Lacking a brood patch, the gannet incubates its egg beneath the webbed feet. For a fortnight or so, the small chick is thinly covered with white down and kept snug beneath a parent. Then the shuttle service with food begins and has a conspicuous effect on the growth of the *guga*. One adult stays on duty; the other ranges far, gathering fish food and returning to regurgitate it, the young gannet thrusting its bill into the gape and taking in a large quantity of the nourishing fish soup. The fledgling period is prolonged. As it comes to a close, the young bird actually has a greater weight than an adult.

Bryan Nelson has referred to 'the traumatic moment in which a juvenile gannet rushes headlong to the cliff edge and jumps, topples or is pushed over or – if it is lucky – jumps off its ledge in its own good time', breaking a fantastically strong tie with the land. At first, that youngster is incapable of flight; it cannot fish for itself and lives on the accumulated fat until these accomplishments are acquired. 'Dishevelled corpses, washed up on the tideline, testify that not all young gannets achieve independence before the fat runs out.'

It does not take long to explore Bass Rock. The hard-surfaced path from near the lighthouse terminates at the foghorn. There are substantial railings beside the path. A small boy, one of the visitors, ran towards the foghorn. Gannets took flight. Hundreds of birds swirled in the air – a sunlit host, white against a deep blue sea. I have since thought of the broken nights spent by birds near the foghorn in poor visibility, when the contraption is bellowing like an amorous bull. And I have recalled those gannets that choose to nest near the lighthouse and must have their eyes seared by the powerful rays. Perhaps, in due course, they will develop an extra eyelid!

Some weeks later, I returned to North Berwick to be taken for a cruise around the smaller islands: The Lamb and Craigleith. Now the problem was a shortage of water. The boatman ruefully admitted that, having failed to take his boat outside the harbour on the ebbing of the tide, he could not move it until the flow was well under way. The harbour had virtually dried out; there was just a glorified puddle near its entrance.

Fidra could be seen in a firth dotted with black rocks. Fidra, connected to the mainland by a reef, was used as a retreat for meditation by the nuns of the Cistercian convent of North Berwick. Close by was The Lamb, while Craigleith, the largest of the trio, stood at a range of little more than a mile from the harbour.

The boat's progress on the still water left a herring-bone pattern and a smudge of fumes from the engine. We passed cormorants, shags and auks to reach The Lamb, a glorified knob of rock that was feathered by birds. There would have been utter confusion among them if we had decided to land. Gull chicks seemed to be in the numerical ascendancy. Many of them were feathered, and some took to the water, possibly for the first time. Cormorants were in flight, using their webbed feet to control their speed and direction. The adults perched near the nests had the regal air of Germanic emblems. Young birds were at the downy stage, though no doubt their wings were beginning to sprout feathers. Their appearance proclaimed a reptilian ancestry. I watched a cormorant delivering some fish stew to its offspring, which thrust its beak into the gape. Twice a day, the growing nestlings receive a helping of this nourishing fare that is derived almost entirely from fish, invariably flat fish, caught on the bed of shallow coastal waters.

The eggs must be protected from gulls. The new-hatched young are covered by an adult to protect them from the sunshine and drying air. On the nest, when the weather is hot, cormorants gape, or their white throats ripple, a cooling device. Young birds which have reached the stage of flight do not cast off dependence on the parents for a considerable time. I watched a cormorant standing with wings outstretched. Another preened, collecting a waterproofing solution from a gland, cleansing the feathers of the slime from captured fish.

On the opposite side of the island, where the cliffs offered broad ledges close to the sea, shags squatted on their untidy nests. The bodies of these birds were sheened by green, the heads adorned with jaunty little crests. The owner of a nest lunged in the direction of the boat, displaying a yellow throat. The guardian shag swayed from side to side, calling in a deep, rasping voice.

A township of shags appeared to view. Birds were swimming, their bodies being so low in the water they were almost awash. A shag that scrambled onto the dark rocks stood briefly with dripping wings, displaying a splash of chrome yellow at the throat. Attached to the blackened mass of nesting material were some bright yellowy-green pieces of fresh vegetation. Shags fish in rather deeper water than that frequented by the cormorants, and free-swimming fish are the chief prey, the bag including sand-eels. With a bountiful sea, the shag can nest virtually anywhere on the coast providing it has a broad ledge, such as at the base of a cliff or in a sea cave. A few guillemots were present. There was no large, rowdy assembly of birds. One chick, with a downy two-tone suit, standing on a rock shelf beside a gully, was in a solitary state and almost at the stage of being able to leave land, which it would do in the twilight of a July evening.

Craigleith, also known as Lamb Island, had its thickets of tree-mallow and congregation of nesting gulls, with large chicks in attendance. In places, the vegetation of this island is varied by wild barley, of cream-yellow hue. The herring-gulls screamed and circled. One year a friend lost his Scottish bonnet to a Craigleith gull. He had landed on the island, and a bird dived so closely that one of its feet was entangled in the wool of the bonnet. The bonnet was carried away!

We sailed near cliffs holding a few puffins, some razorbills, a company of shags – and gulls. Then the skipper set course for North Berwick, anxious to tie up his boat before the harbour dried out.

# 17

# Mull of Galloway: Razorbills and Butterflies

Terns were plunge-diving in the Nith, a few miles below Dumfries. Wavering spume marked the division between river and sea, and the birds were on the salty side of the line. A man was fishing in the old Norse way, using a purse-net on a frame. He stood a few paces from the bank, but nonetheless the water came up to his chest.

I was on my way to the Mull of Galloway, the most southerly point in Scotland, but I found the haaf-netter's ancient skills so exciting that I watched him until a fish nosed its way into the net. The fisherman could not see it, but he felt the vibration and lifted the cumbersome structure clear of the water. Two flounders – floundered! To one who was seeking salmon, there was no cause for rejoicing. He grunted. The flounders were lately spawned and therefore inedible.

The fisherman tossed one fish against my boots, and I watched fascinated as it flip-flopped its way back into the river. Forty licences are issued for haaf-nets in this area, and a system of tallies ensures fairness when the men select their positions. This man had an hour, no more, in which to intercept a salmon. He carried a wooden truncheon, known as a 'priest', since it is used to administer the last rites when a takeable fish is killed.

The terns nested on the large merse across the water. Scores of flickering wings were to be seen against a backdrop provided by stern Criffel, a hill that is nowhere near the 2,000-feet mark needed for mountain status but one that makes a strong visual impact on the northern shore of Solway. With a flow tide, the terns faced the sea. Water and fish passed swiftly beneath them. The fisherman estimated the speed of the tide at about six knots, so a bird looked well ahead of the point at which it hovered. Its head was set at a downward angle, and the dagger-like beak, blood-red, was poised for action. The bird plunged. Water spurted. The bird rose, unsuccessful, and shook itself in the air before resuming its vigil. Another bird headed towards the merse with a silver fish held crossways in its beak.

The terns had a streamlined grace; they were light, buoyant, always alert. Six terns at a time were spaced out, above the river, their eyes fixed on the salty side of that wavering line of spume. A bird dived with half-closed wings; another bird hovered, and yet another flew low as though assessing the prospects. At a guess, the prey item that day was whitebait.

The liveliness of the terns compensated me for the rain and mist that cocooned the road for the whole hundred miles from Gretna to the Rhinns of Galloway. I followed the meandering of the A75 westwards through Annan, Dumfries and Creetown. There were weary miles of wet tarmac and sheets of spray from other traffic, in an area where normally the journey is a pleasant part of the outing to the famous Mull. At other times, I had enjoyed the slow unwinding of a varied landscape, with the sea never far away.

I eventually left the misty moorland and the main road to cross a flange of low ground that tethers the Rhinns to the mainland. Look at a map: it gives the impression of an island in the last stages of evolution. I travelled between the conifers of a commercial plantation, and then I really felt to be in Old Galloway, with a deciduous-mix. It was humid now, the air scented by flowers, though what little I saw of the sea was grey and languid under mist. Luce Bay was no more inspiring than bathwater.

My spirits revived as the sky brightened. Excited oystercatchers performed a bizarre ballet, several of them advancing – at times in line-ahead formation, and at times side by side – with their heads down, red bills almost scraping the ground, feet in stamping movement, and their shrill cries reflecting their ecstasy as they pursued a female. I took it to be a female. The bird ran briskly ahead, looking more alarmed than excited. Two mute swans, cruising near the beach, had a snow-goose for company. It was undoubtedly a snow-goose, with pink bill, white plumage and a hint of black at the tips of the furled wings. The water was clear and calm enough for me to see the bird's pink feet. The matey snow-goose was turned upon by the swans; they peevishly hissed at it.

The foliage of deciduous trees, and the fronds of bracken on the hillside, were prematurely aged by salt water that had been tossed over them by a recent tempestuous sea. Yet there was a profusion of roadside flowers, including red campion and meadow cranesbill. Galloway's balmy climate was evident from the sight of a grove of tree-mallow near a cottage.

A salmon fisherman, having hung out a salmon bag-net to dry, was plucking from it any stray pieces of weed. Such a net is regarded as a 'fixed engine', being normally left in the sea for days. The salmon swim between leaders to enter what is in effect a cage. This man had caught only nine salmon that season.

He was familiar with Luce Bay, of course. I asked him about the Scar Rocks, a nesting place of the gannet. They were an hour's sail away, and he had been there often. Scar Rocks are almost fifty miles from Ailsa Craig, in the Clyde, from which the 'founding fathers' of the colony must have come. The fisherman drew me a sketch of two small islands, on which the grey seals haul them-selves to doze and sunbathe, and of the big rock – over 60 feet in height, and some 300 feet long, composed of schist with some quartz. The comparatively few gannets have precarious nest-ing sites here, but they are isolated, safe from land-based pre-dators, except man, and with some excellent fishing all around them.

Drummore post office proudly announced itself as 'the first or last in Scotland'. The landscape began to take on an Irish charac-ter, with small, hedge-bordered fields lying on a series of gentle undulations. Irish crofter-fishermen settled this area fifteen cen-turies ago, after a pitched battle with the Picts. The people who arrived from Ulster were, of course, the original Scots.

I drove along a narrow road, between verges bright with summer flowers. A light breeze ran a comb through fields of barley, much of which would be fed to the cattle. On my first visit, many years ago, I photographed a thatched cottage, and now I looked for it in vain. Perhaps it was the roofless structure I noticed beside the road. A track led me to a sheltered part of the coast, where lobster-pots were stacked, the base of each pot incorporat-ing a rough block of concrete as ballast. The area around Scar Rocks is prime lobster ground.

Glaswegians on holiday had parked their cars half a mile further on. From here they had a short walk to the edge of the sea, where they were fishing from a steep rock, casting their lines over a bed of kelp to reach a sandy bottom where mackerel were on the move.

A man jubilantly displayed fifty mackerel and one pollack, all captured on unbaited hooks. He had simply adorned the hooks with red feathers to attract the mackerels' curiosity. Luce Bay mackerels were once advertised as such. 'They're guid,' I was told by a man who liked to grill the fish, having first spread English mustard over it. The 'fire' in the mustard was lost during the cooking. Mackerel are 'too greasy' to be fried, he asserted. Sometimes he barbecued them, and at home he also had a 'wee smoker'. He was, without doubt, an expert on mackerel. The fish I saw were in good condition, though I fancied that they had died with a baleful look in their eyes, as though aware – at the moment before death – of the cruel trick that had been played upon them. Unbaited hooks, indeed!

I drove back into the mist. On the Mull of Galloway, the foghorn's mournful aria was to be heard – a sound resembling the deep, dry voice of the bittern. The horn comes into operation when visibility is less than three miles. Seabirds nesting nearby soon accept the thunderous double-notes, after an initial panic that sends many of them careering over the sea. I parked on short grass, near a puddle that was large enough to be designated as a lochan. A bullock emerged from the mist and sniffed at the hot bonnet of the car. The foghorn continued its Wagnerian lament. The rest was silence, apart from my rhythmic champing of sandwiches and my occasional heartfelt sighs.

Do you recall the transformation scene at a pantomime – the moment when the curtains swish back after an interval to reveal not only light and colour but some great, multi-coloured novelty? That is the sort of experience I had at the Mull of Galloway. The west wind had strengthened. I became aware of patches of blue, high in the sky. The mist thinned to reveal reddish cliffs that were up to 200 feet high; they sloped backwards, as though they were taking the strain of the whole of Scotland. Now the lower part of the sixty-foot lighthouse was gleaming as it caught the eye of the sun. The last wraithes went by, and Luce Bay was in view – azure, with a fishing boat as insignificant as a water-beetle. I could easily see the Lakeland hills.

Kittiwakes gave a round of calling, as though celebrating the return of summer. (It was mid-July). Rocks, encrusted with lichen, were so brightly illuminated by the sun I had the impression that someone had splashed them with iodine. The sea sparkled. A blue butterfly soaked up the warmth and strong light.

My car lay at the edge of grassland which sheep had mown to the fineness of a lawn. I gingerly crossed a cattle grid, passing through a gap in the high wall that marks out the domain of the Northern Lights, forty acres of which are leased as a reserve by the RSPB. No farm stock had worked out the technique of crossing the cattle grid as have some sheep on the Pennines. Within the walled area – this tip of the Mull of Galloway, this southernmost few acres of Scotland – I could see what nature is capable of when she is left alone.

The ling was dull and brown as yet, though a foretaste of its regal splendour when flowering was provided by clumps of bell heather which stood up jauntily, holding out arms full of purple bloom. Mountain milk-vetch was here at its only location in the south of Scotland. Tormentil was in lusty growth. Thyme soaked up the sunlight. White campion and sea pink testified to the maritime nature of the area.

Common blue butterflies, two or three at a time, flickered over the grass. A large hairy caterpillar rested on the path I followed to reach the tip of the headland. So dry were the conditions that grasshoppers provided an instrumental accompaniment to my walk. The summer sea looked uneasy. Ebbing tide, rocks and a westerly breeze set up a line of white-capped waves and created whirlpools in a limited area. Nine tides are said to meet off the Mull of Galloway.

There were few seabirds, but they were easy to observe. They did not overwhelm a visitor by sheer force of numbers. I felt I could have got to know each bird as an individual. A black speck over the sea was a razorbill in hectic flight. Then it was close enough for the fine detail to be taken in. The bird braked furiously, setting its body close to the vertical, trapping the air with wings and webbed feet. Other razorbills appeared, on a similar course, flashing out of sight near the foghorn. So I went there and sat on the rock. The razorbills zoomed by, but not before they had displayed their black heads and those curious, laterally compressed bills. The feet that acted as air-brakes were dark grey in colour. Far out, other razorbills moved, fast and direct, their plump bodies shaped like torpedoes, their relatively small wings moving so quickly to sustain the size and weight of the bird that they were blurred to my vision.

The razorbill is a bird that needs the lift provided by the wind. In calm conditions it treads water for a while before it has attained a speed at which it can fly clear of the sea. When leaving the nesting site, a razorbill tends to make a steep descent. When you fancy it is about to dash itself against the rocks or water, the fluttering wings bring it to an adequate speed for level flight. An artist friend captured this with a touch of novelty. I took him to a seabird cliff, and he painted lots of birds, not in recognisable forms but according to the height and manner of flight. He including swirling white lines for kittiwakes and the dark, descending, then rising streaks that were the flight paths of the auks.

This was the largest concentration of razorbills I had actually seen. The book told me that more were present in other places, but either the cliffs were too large or the birds were too secretive to attract notice to themselves. The cliffs of the Mull of Galloway have many a nook and cranny, and also some boulder slopes, to attract razorbills. The guillemots I saw were of the brown southern race; when my head broke the skyline near one group, the uneasy birds moved their heads in excitement, and agitation led some of them to plunge into the sea. Some guillemots brooded quite large chicks. The piping calls of anxious young birds joined the deep growling of the adults.

Razorbills and butterflies; red rocks and a sparkling sea – these were the main impressions I carried away with me from the Mull of Galloway. I gingerly crossed the cattle grid as yet another blue butterfly went by . . .

I motored northwards, close to the Clyde. Horse Island, off Ardrossan, was low against a series of foam-crested waves. The isle is less than a mile in length and under 300 yards wide but has nesting terns – terns of four species, which add grating calls to the general din. And here the butterflies also have the company of gulls! From Girvan, Ailsa Craig looked like an upturned pudding-basin. The main ornithological glory of the island – a gannetry that was first mentioned just 400 years ago – is to be found on the western and southern sides. Some 16,000 pairs of gannets look like a huge white crescent resting on its back.

Ailsa Craig is so dominant in its watery setting that Irishmen emigrating to Glasgow nicknamed it 'Paddy's Milestone'. The Craig (as locals call it) resembles Bass Rock in several respects, but it is further from the mainland. Distance does not rob it of its grandeur. A close view of the gannetry, from the sea, is a memory to cherish.

I hired a boat at Girvan and was taken across a bumpy sea to The Craig. We approached under clouds of battleship grey, but the sky behind the rock brightened; then the clouds parted for half an hour and let the sunshine through. The boatmen and I saw the gannetry in its full glory. Rising from a narrow, rocky beach were cliffs that soared to over a thousand feet. They extended well beyond the normal field of vision, so that I had to bend my neck backwards to see the top.

The rock was curiously fluted or twisted, and Ailsa's impressive height was accentuated by its mirror-like reflection in the sea. Gannets flew from the whitened ledges. Dozens of gannets became hundreds of gannets. Soon half the sky was speckled with birds that were backlit by the sun, resembling whirring fragments from a fire.

Keats wrote of The Craig:

> *Hearken, thou craggy ocean-pyramid!*
> *Give answer from thy voice, the sea-fowl's scream!*

And later:

> *Thy life is but two dead eternities –*
> *The last in air, the former in the deep;*
> *First with the whales, last with the eagle-skies*
> *Drown'd wast thou till an earthquake made thee steep:*
> *Another cannot wake thy giant size.*

# 18

# The Solway: Whooping Swans and Arctic Geese

Could they really be wild, these whooper swans that passed over my head at a height of no more than fifty feet? The birds called; their wings produced a whistling sound. I walked between earthen banks and rows of bare thorntrees, pausing whenever I heard the bugle-like notes – *whoop-a-whoop, whoop-a-whoop*. A family group passed over me, white bodies underlit by the morning sunlight, wings beating with shallow strokes that nonetheless had considerable power.

The setting was Caerlaverock, on the Scottish shore of the Solway Firth. I stood at the edge of one of the largest salt marshes in western Britain, not far from the Inner Solway, a tract of mud, sand and churning water, the third largest inter-tidal area in the kingdom, providing prime feeding areas for waders and ducks as well as safe roosts for the wintering geese.

I was visiting Eastpark, a property of the Wildfowl Trust. Over a hundred wild whoopers, refugees from Iceland, and a considerably smaller number of Bewick's swans from Siberia, had been attracted to its ponds. Other swans were scattered about the commodious merse. Whoopers passed in pairs or small family parties. The beaks of the mature birds were yellow, tipped with black. The dusky young were as yet grey on the upper beak.

Birds came near to brushing the topmost branches of the thorns, from which a few scarlet berries dangled. The sky was a duck-egg blue, the air slack and warm. Near the Solway, the sky occupies two-thirds of every view. As I approached Eastpark, I was overtaken by a skein of pink-footed geese – a single, wavering chevron holding almost a hundred birds.

On acquiring Eastpark, the Trust reared several miles of earthen banks. From a hide set into one of these man-made ridges, I overlooked a series of ponds that had appeared when earth was excavated for the banking. A whooper pair and five young birds were feeding here, and on the stubble of the flat field over 2,000 barnacle geese had assembled.

At any given moment, dozens of geese gave voice, and so there was a constant babbling: a wild babbling, as befits the calls of birds that nest in the Arctic. So lush were the undersown grasses that the geese grazed in a large block that scarcely moved. Five greylags appeared, circled and wiffled to touch down beyond the barnacle throng. Over 600 pink-footed geese stirred on Solway shore. These birds had enjoyed several hours of feeding under a full moon before they assembled at a safe roosting place to rest and preen.

The merse at Caerlaverock covers 51,500 acres; it extends from Kenneth Bank to the mouth of the Lockar Water. The National Nature Reserve incorporates 12,000 acres of the foreshore – basically the feature known as Blackshaw Bank – and so the roosting area of the geese is protected. It is also an important feeding area for waders and ducks.

My gaze returned to the whooper swans. The male stood apart from the others. Its neck was upstretched, as straight as a poker. Every movement of the head indicated alertness. It is the male's job to be alert, said the warden of the reserve, who joined me in the hide. The female, though watchful, tends to be in the immediate presence of the young birds. As ever, I was impressed by the robust nature of the whooper swans. They had nested in Iceland and migrated to their wintering grounds entirely over water – across some 500 miles of the stormy North Atlantic.

By two o'clock, a movement to the main ponds had begun. Whoopers were dropping below the line of wooden buildings overlooking those ponds. Birds descended with excited calls as they joined the main assembly. Entering the buildings, I walked around a partition that acts as a baffle, providing a dark background to the viewing area. The moment at which the ponds came into view was memorable. A series of large windows gave unimpeded viewing. In the hard, clear sunlight swam a host of snow-white swans – whooper, Bewick's, mute. I had to remind myself that these were wild, free-flying birds. How many of them had seen a human being until their British landfall? Now, on the Eastpark reserve, they swam in a gleaming white mass, not exactly jostling each other – though one or two brief disputes occurred – but in such numbers that I half-expected to see water lapping over the sides of the pond.

The whoopers remained in their family groups. In the previous winter, a maximum of 129 whoopers was recorded at Eastpark, and already, before the end of 1982, the number had risen to 150. Whoopers tend to move a great deal. In winter, as many as 200 individuals might visit this Solway sanctuary. The warden provides a ration of barley each day, and so visitors to the reserve see some of the waterfowl at close quarters. Ornithologists marvel that birds from a boreal wilderness are swimming within a few feet of the big windows. (Even the 'wary wigeon' can be seen swimming close by, and shoveller, pochard, gadwall, mallard and teal all frequent the pond.)

A whooper lumbered onto the shore on black-webbed feet and delicately picked at the grains of barley. This bird carried a yellow ring, on which a number had been stamped. A check could be made on its movements. Some swans have a picric acid dye daubed on their tails, and the bright yellow can be seen half a parish away. It does not harm the swans and vanishes during the next moult; meanwhile, more information is assembled on the nomadic nature of the whooper swan. Until the marking scheme began, it was presumed that all the swans came from Iceland, where the nesting population is now about 5,000 pairs. All but a few hundred birds migrate to Britain for the winter. Then one of the 'yellow-tails' from Eastpark was seen at Tallin, in northern Russia, and the whooper study took on a new dimension.

Autumn brings ducks from a wide area of northern Europe. Up to 2,500 pintail alight on the barley stubbles in October. There may be over 1,000 wigeon in the area, with rather more than half that number of mallard and some 800 teal. A host of birds, refugees from the far-northern winter, arrives in a district that, in summer, seemed empty. On a summer visit, I saw cattle wandering across the face of the marsh or cropping succulent grasses. The merse was built up over two or three centuries, having a base of sand and silt washed in from the bed of the Irish Sea by the restless tides. In summer, the shelduck, having nested in rabbit burrows at the back of the merse, were taking their striped youngsters to water. Redshank rose from the creeks, shouting alarm; lapwings flew around on their tufty wings, and snipe leapt with a succession of sneezes from the most boggy areas.

The merse flowers bountifully. There may be several thousand spikes of the northern marsh orchid in an area called The Flooders. The big fields inland may have been ploughed and re-seeded or planted with cereal crops, but there is a linear nature reserve in the hedgerows: drifts of bluebells, gorse in golden bloom, thorns holding out arms full of white blossom which is complemented by the white of cow parsley at the roadsides.

Caerlaverock may be flat; the dun-coloured desert of the Solway may lack prominent details, and the skies are vast, but this southern rim of Scotland has its conspicuous hill, Criffel, which rises to a little over 1,800 feet, and in the context of the Grampians it would be overlooked and yet, in its isolated position, to the west of the Nith estuary, shouts to be noticed. The ruins of Caerlaverock Castle provide nesting places for jackdaw, swallow, kestrel and barn owl; there are mallard and Chinese geese in the moat. The fox is seen trotting across the merse, a roe deer flits about the scene at the 'edge o' dark', when it seems but a little more substantial than a shadow. Several years ago, the mink appeared . . .

Languid summer fades into autumn. The air-lanes become busy as the wildfowl of northern latitudes move towards their temperate wintering areas. About mid-September, watchers by the Solway scan the sky for the first viewing of immigrant geese, pink-footed geese, back from their nesting areas in Iceland. A small group of birds – fifteen or twenty – appear. Another day, many more geese are seen. Freshly arrived birds rest on the banks for a few hours and then spread out to feed on rough ground and on the quieter farms. Waders by the tens of thousands are like brown clouds drifting along the tideline. Knot and golden plover, dunlin and bar-tailed godwit feed at the edge of the sea or spread themselves across the merse.

By late September, the main party of Spitzbergen barnacle geese has crossed the North Sea and the south-east coast of Scotland, flying to Caerlaverock, to complete a migratory flight of some 1,800 miles. Within a fortnight, all the geese are in their wintering area. The same impulse to move has directed barnacles from Greenland to winter-quarters in Ireland and on the Western Isles. Flocks of barnacles from Novaya Zemlya, in Russia, sojourn in the Low Countries. The geese from different nesting areas do not intermingle.

Early in the winter, barnacle geese may be found grazing close up to the hides of Eastpark. Many more are spread across the merse. The barnacle is relatively small and dapper, handsomely marked with black, white and grey. The face is white; the crown and neck are black, creating a nun-like appearance. These 'black geese' of the Solway nest only 700 miles from the North Pole. The Spitzbergen nesting grounds are clear of snow and ice for only four months of the year, and the spring thaw reveals an austere landscape in which mosses and lichen adorn the frost-shattered rocks. Coastal marshes are patches of green against the dark, snow-ribbed mountains.

During the nesting season, immature birds familiarise themselves with this bleak environment. The adults select nesting sites on islets where, hopefully, they cannot be reached by the Arctic foxes. The eggs are laid in a small depression that has been lagged with moss and lichen and, eventually, with down. For a few days after hatching, the young birds are vulnerable to predation by glaucous gulls; then the parent geese swim with their young to the bogs and Arctic pastures on the low ground by the coast.

By August, the adults have gone into the moult, and the young are flightless, too, in the process of acquiring their shining first plumage. In September, with the days shortening fast, groups of birds head for the Norwegian coast, where some will rest and graze on offshore islands, and others make the formidable journey to Caerlaverock without stopping. An excited babbling tells the watchers by the Solway that the barnacles are back. They normally come from the north-east, but birds may be taken by a gale far to the west, and they approach by way of the Nith valley or even eastwards, up the Solway itself. As with the whooper swans, we keep a check on the movement of some birds by marking them. Rocket-netting is the means to this end, and the captured birds are daubed with dye. I saw some 'yellow-tails', also a white barnacle, a local celebrity.

The warden at Eastpark had summed up the temperament of the barnacle geese as 'noisy, restless, chattering, highly-strung and extremely wary'. His assessment was borne out by the behaviour of the birds I watched; they did not fly but were alert to every strange sound and movement. Necks were raised, heads vigorously shaken. If alarmed, the birds stand for a second or two, trembling like tuning-forks, and then they are away, pouring over the embankments to fresh grazing areas. You will find them grazing at Caerlaverock, on the shore near Southerness, and at the tip of Rockcliffe Marsh, across the Solway.

Numerically, these Spitzbergen barnacle geese have their dramatic ups and downs. It has long been so. It is guesstimated that early this century between 8,000 and 10,000 geese were wintering by the Solway; the numbers declined as wildfowling became more popular, and in the 1930s the geese had a series of poor nesting seasons. Came the war, and Caerlaverock merse was used as a bombing range! By the 1940s, the barnacle population was down to about 300 birds, and the species was given legal protection. A National Nature Reserve was established, and in 1970 the Wildfowl Trust set up its reserve at Eastpark to study the geese, to conserve the stocks by providing sanctuary and good feeding and to make arrangements for the public to see the geese without disturbing them.

Good breeding seasons during the 1970s assisted the bird's numerical recovery. The population peaked at 9,050 in October, 1980. In that year, 23 per cent of young birds were recorded at Caerlaverock. Yet these small and lively geese remain vulnerable to the Arctic weather. In the following season, when snow and ice were slow to clear from the nesting grounds, the figure had dropped to 3 per cent.

By day, the barnacle geese graze on grasses and seeds. An important source of food is the stolon of the white clover, which is rich in starch. The shoots extend horizontally from the main plant. Cattle, in their summer grazing of the merse, ensure that the grass does not become long and rank. Watching the barnacle geese, I became aware of the strong group spirit to which the warden had referred and to his observation that the mass of geese was actually a collection of many groups. A gander attempts to hold its own feeding territory, and if another bird intrudes, it is chased away, the home bird stabbing its bill in the air as it moves threateningly towards the intruder. By spreading their grazing over three major sites, the geese ensure that the food supply will last.

At dusk, the birds roost on mudflats, one or two miles from land. The arrival of a flow tide during the roosting period means that for an hour or two the birds will be afloat. The return of the barnacle geese to land at dawn is spectacular if all the birds are assembled, for well over 8,000 bodies occupy a lot of sky. The birds also fill the air with their wild chattering.

Half-light is a magical time by the Solway in winter. The musical calls of the pink-footed geese, heralding their approach, carry for a mile or two in still weather. The birds climb as they approach land, so that when they cross the coast they are beyond the range of wildfowlers' guns. Some distance inland, they circle and wiffle, touching down in areas they know from experience to be safe. Grey geese often leave the firth over Brow Well, and the chevrons and lines create futuristic patterns in the sky. A passage of geese may take ten minutes or an hour; their density varies from morning to morning. The barnacles fly in a merry throng of chattering birds, or there may be several large groups.

The departure for the nesting grounds, in mid to late April, tends to be inconspicuous. Most of the barnacle geese are on the point of Rockcliffe, beyond the ken of watchers on the main shoreline. They move off surreptitiously, in the early morning, setting their course to the north-east, breaking their journey at a group of islands off the Norwegian coast where, for a week or two, they graze, laying on fat for the second half of their journey. They must reach Spitzbergen in peak condition.

After that, it is up to the weather. Every day counts in the Arctic nesting season . . .

# Some Other Bird Haunts

*Islay: Wild Geese by the Thousand*
Barnacle geese of Greenland origin, even more numerous than those frequenting Caerlaverock, may be seen in winter on 'the green isle'. At times, the barnacle flock exceeds 20,000. Winter days see other visitors from Greenland, some 2,500 white-fronted geese. The number sometimes reaches 5,000.

These are but two of many species of bird that frequent the most southerly island of the Inner Hebrides: a large island, 25 miles from north to south, 20 miles from east to west. It is nearly dissected by Lochs Gruinart and Indaal. This is no wild, rocky island but one that lives up to the name 'green island', with a well-established and large farming community and no less than eight distilleries.

Islay can be visited by air from Glasgow or by car-ferry from West Loch Tarbert, on the Mull of Kintyre. The Islay, Jura and Colonsay Tourist Association has its headquarters at the largest place, Bowmore, and a bird list can be obtained from the Islay Folk Museum.

Islay has scenic variety, and an impressive list of nesting and wintering birds. Black guillemots bob on the waves off the rocky parts of the shore. Red-throated divers cruise on the lochs. The chough is at home here. Terns and eiders nest on offshore islets.

*Orkney: Nesting Birds and Standing Stones*
It is an impertinence to write of the avian wonders of Orkney in a small note. Whole books could be – and have been! – written about this cluster of sixty islands lying a mere seven miles from the north coast of Scotland. They are in three large groups – North Isles, Mainland and South Isles. An air service operates to Kirkwall, and as with Shetland, inter-island air travel is possible. If you would like to take a car to Orkney, then the P & O ferry

operating from Scrabster to Stromness will accommodate it. An excursion to Orkney is also a journey into pre-history. The islands abound with evidence of early settlement, including some impressive standing stones.

The bird-watcher, spoilt for choice, would do well to read up about the bird habitats in advance. Notable haunts are now reserves of the RSPB, so you can, if you are a member, consult the list of reserves and visiting arrangements; if not a member, write with a stamped envelope to the Scottish office of the Society at 17 Regent Terrace, Edinburgh EH7 5BN. And also ask for membership details! Information about Orkney, and a leaflet on the bird life, are available from the Orkney Tourist Office, Broad Street, Kirkwall.

The Noup Cliffs, Westray, are accessible at all times. Here you will come close to being deafened by the cries of seabirds, including an estimated 40,000 guillemots and 25,000 pairs of kittiwakes. Further massive congregations are seen on the Old Red Sandstone of Marwick Head, near Dounby, to which there is access at all times along a path that runs northwards from Marwick Bay.

Orkney is generally well farmed. A prime tract of moorland, and yet another RSPB reserve, is at Hobbister, near Kirkwall, where the little Orkney vole tries to live a life of its own and is regarded as protein-packed-in-fur by predators such as hen-harriers and short-eared owls. Of the former, there may be five nesting females. The moorland also holds merlins, nesting waders and red grouse.

Papa Westray's North Hill is wardened. The warden, who lives in a local cottage, likes to hear in advance of impending visits. The address is c/o Gowrie, Papa Westray, Orkney KW17 2BU. The whole island, only four miles long by a mile wide, actually has its own air link. The sky clouds with Arctic terns. Corncrakes do their celebrated disappearing-act in the long vegetation. Arctic skuas dart about the moors with mewing calls. Black guillemots bob like two-tone buoys on the sea.

The island of Copinsay, to which there is access at all times, can be visited by excursion boat from Skaill or the west end of Newark Bay. Copinsay was purchased as a memorial to the late James Fisher. Though small, the island has plenty of avian interest. Cliffs on the south-eastern side, rising to 200 feet, provide nesting sites for auks, kittiwakes and shags. Arctic terns nest on Corn Holm.

## Outer Hebrides: the Western Rim of Europe

They are known collectively as The Long Island, these islands of all shapes and sizes that form a chain from the Butt of Lewis to Barra, or if you wish from North Rona to Ailsa Craig. Linked to the Scottish mainland by air services and car-ferries, the Western Isles have that atmosphere of remoteness and austerity that lends enchantment to those who do not know them and who, making a first visit, move excitedly from one novel feature to another.

North Uist, an island 12 miles by 16 miles – and rather less mountainous than South Uist – has an abundance of lochs, attractive to visiting anglers. For the bird-watcher, it has a prime bird reserve, Balranald, where the local celebrites are greylag geese, corncrakes, red-necked phalarope, shoveller and tufted duck and an abundance of waders. Gannets and shearwaters may be seen off shore. The visitor should contact the summer warden at the reception cottage, Goular (not Balranald), near Houghharry, Lochmaddy.

The Western Isles Tourist Organisation has its headquarters at 4 South Beach Street, Stornoway.

## St Kilda: Mountains in the Ocean

This celebrated group of islands, lying some 50 miles west of Harris, is not easy of access. Sometimes excursions are organised, tourists being taken on a voyage around the island group without landing. Those wishing to land or to join a working party must contact the National Trust for Scotland, who have owned the island since 1957, when it was bequeathed to them by the Marquess of Bute. That same year, a military tracking station was established on Hirta. The islands are leased for field studies to the Nature Conservancy Council.

The 'bird people' of St Kilda have been referred to elsewhere. The setting for this former community of self-reliant people is made for superlatives. St Kilda, also known as Hirta, rises to 1,400 feet, having the highest sheer sea cliff in Britain. Other major islands are Boreray, Dun and Soay. Stac Lee is an impressive 564-foot rock. The air above St Kilda is clouded with seabirds during the nesting season.

*Strathbeg: A Loch Beside the Sea*

The Loch of Strathbeg is one of Britain's most important haunts of wildfowl. Extending to over 490 acres, it lies between Peterhead and Fraserburgh. A crucial factor is that the water is relatively shallow, around five feet, and is surrounded by calcareous dunes. The loch is rich in nutrients and has an abundance of submerged vegetation. It lies a mere half mile from the open sea.

Large numbers of grey geese roost here in winter, when there is also a sizeable herd of whooper swans, with a few Bewick's swans. (This is, indeed, the most northerly haunt of Bewick's in Britain.) On my last visit I was impressed by the many eiders and saw fulmars swimming on the calm water, out of sight of the sea.

The Loch is an RSPB Reserve, by arrangement with the owners. It is open the year through, on Wednesdays and Sundays; you will need a permit in advance from the warden, who lives at The Lythe, Crimonmogate, Lonmay, Fraserburgh.

While in this area, visit the Ythan estuary. Bird-watching is relatively easy from the nearby roads. The extensive sand dunes of Forvie are a National Nature Reserve and the breeding place of about 2,000 eiders and many terns, including Sandwich terns.

# Some Useful Addresses

Caledonian MacBrayne Ltd, The Pier, Gourock, Strathclyde.

Highlands and Isles Development Board, 27 Bank Street, Inverness IV1 1QR.

Loganair Ltd, St Andrew's Drive, Glasgow Airport, Glasgow.

National Trust for Scotland, 5 Charlotte Square, Edinburgh EH2 4DU.

Nature Conservancy Council, Scottish Office, 12 Hope Street, Edinburgh 9.

Northern Lighthouse Board, George Street, Edinburgh.

P and O Ferries Ltd, PO Box 5, Aberdeen.

Royal Society for the Protection of Birds, The Lodge, Sandy, Bedfordshire. Scottish Office: 17 Regent Terrace, Edinburgh, EH7 5BN.

Scottish Ornithologists' Club, 21 Regent Terrace, Edinburgh 7.

Scottish Tourist Board, 23 Ravelston Terrace, Edinburgh.

Western Isles Tourist Organisation, 4 South Beach Street, Stornoway.

# Index